# HOTSPOTS
# MADE

**Written by Marc di Duca**
Original photography by Marc di Duca
Front cover photography by Harry Horton/Pictures Colour Library
Series design based on an original concept by Studio 183 Limited

**Produced by Cambridge Publishing Management Limited**
Project Editor: Alison Coupe
Layout: Donna Pedley
Maps: PCGraphics (UK) Ltd

**Published by Thomas Cook Publishing**
A division of Thomas Cook Tour Operations Limited
Company Registration No. 1450464 England
PO Box 227, Coningsby Road
Peterborough PE3 8SB, United Kingdom
email: books@thomascook.com
www.thomascookpublishing.com
+ 44 (0) 1733 416477

ISBN: 978-1-84157-810-1

**First edition © 2007 Thomas Cook Publishing**
Text © 2007 Thomas Cook Publishing
Maps © 2007 Thomas Cook Publishing
Project Editor: Diane Ashmore
Production/DTP Editor: Steven Collins

Printed and bound in Spain by GraphyCems

# CONTENTS

## WHAT'S IN YOUR GUIDEBOOK?

**Independent authors** Impartial up-to-date information from our travel experts who meticulously source local knowledge.

**Experience** Thomas Cook's 165 years in the travel industry and guidebook publishing enriches every word with expertise you can trust.

**Travel know-how** Contributions by thousands of staff around the globe, each one living and breathing travel.

**Editors** Travel-publishing professionals, pulling everything together to craft a perfect blend of words, pictures, maps and design.

**You, the traveller** We deliver a practical, no-nonsense approach to information, geared to how you really use it.

○ *João Gonçalves Zarco discovered Madeira*

# INTRODUCTION
Getting to know Madeira

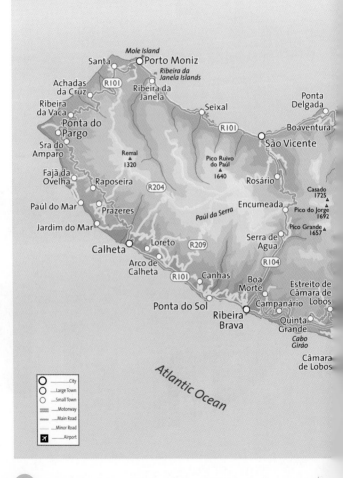

**Map Legend:**

- ○ City
- ○ Large Town
- ○ Small Town
- Motorway
- Main Road
- Minor Road
- ✈ Airport

*Atlantic Ocean*

Mole Island
Porto Moniz
Santa
*Ribeira da Janela Islands*
Achadas da Cruz
R101
Ribeira da Janela
Seixal
Ponta Delgada
Ribeira da Vaça
Ponta do Pargo
R101
Boaventura
São Vicente
Sra do Amparo
Remal 1320
Pico Ruivo do Paúl 1640
Fajã da Ovelha
Raposeira
R204
Rosário
Casado 1725
Paúl do Mar
Prazeres
*Paúl da Serra*
Encumeada
Pico do Jorge 1692
Jardim do Mar
Pico Grande 1657
Calheta
Loreto
R209
Serra de Agua
R104
Arco de Calheta
R101
Canhas
Boa Morte
Estreito de Câmara de Lobos
Ponta do Sol
Ribeira Brava
Campanário
Quinta Grande
*Cabo Girão*
Câmara de Lobos

Madeira

# Getting to know Madeira

Those in search of a holiday destination with year-round sunshine, a soothingly mild climate, heaps of spectacular natural beauty, dramatic landscapes, amazing plant life, easy-going locals and delicious seafood should look no further than the island of Madeira. Although this tiny head of rock in the Atlantic, just 58 km (36 miles) long and 23 km (14 miles) wide, has virtually no sandy beaches, this is more than made up for by great walking trails through the mountainous centre and along the famous *levadas* – manmade channels which bring water from the interior down to the plantations and towns by the coast. If it's a beach holiday you are looking for, Madeira's smaller, older and lesser-known sibling island, Porto Santo, boasts a glorious stretch of golden sand along its south coast and is often described as Europe's best-kept holiday secret. Combine all this with Madeira's superb public transport system, the island's delicious fortified wines, a traditionally high standard of accommodation, gentle sightseeing in the capital, Funchal, and a tourist industry which combines classic development and comfort with unspoilt villages, traditional markets and colourful festivals, and you have what must be one of the most relaxing holiday destinations on the planet.

Madeira was formed 20 million years ago when volcanic eruptions thrust this chunk of rock above the waves of the Atlantic. This unstable,

### FUNCHAL'S MOST FAMOUS SON?

Cristiano Ronaldo dos Santos Aveiro was born in Funchal in February 1985. If the name doesn't ring any bells, you're probably not a football (soccer) fan, as Cristiano Ronaldo (as he is known for short) is currently one of the game's star players and a Portuguese international. His career started at local team Nacional before being transferred to Sporting Lisbon and then Manchester United, where he plies his trade to this day. It is said he is named after Ronald Reagan!

porous volcanic rock was quickly chiselled away by the elements into craggy mountains, deep gorges and dramatic valleys. Precipitous cliffs ring the island such as those at Cabo Girão, some of the highest in the world. Madeira's principal settlements naturally grew up where the land allowed – around the flat mouths of rivers where bays had formed. The highest peaks on the island can be found north of Funchal where Pico Ruivo, Pico das Torres and Pico do Areeiro rise to over 1,800 m (5, 906 ft), and the only flat area inland is the Paúl de Serra plateau in the west. Madeira's volcanic eruptions ran out of steam thousands of years ago, but the island does experience regular minor seismic tremors which locals claim they no longer even notice.

The islanders often describe themselves as Madeirans first and Portuguese second, though the vast majority of Madeira's population originate from mainland Portugal. The only exceptions are those of British stock, fair-haired descendants of merchant families who dominated the sugar and wine trade in centuries past. You will find most Madeirans amiable, polite, and with a certain reserve appreciated by British visitors. The official language is Portuguese, though many in Funchal speak adequate English.

● *The yellow sands of Porto Santo beach*

# THE BEST OF MADEIRA

Despite being a pint-sized islet as far as islands go, Madeira is brimming with countless great things to see and do. From Funchal's historical centre to the wilds of the mountains, from the beaches of Porto Santo to a vibrant early morning market scene, this island never fails to delight.

## TOP 10 ATTRACTIONS

- **Funchal, Madeira's capital city** The epicentre of life on the island and the only major town with 125,000 inhabitants (see page 15).

- **The sandy beaches of Porto Santo** When you feel the light golden sand of Porto Santo's beach between your toes, you'll appreciate why this volcanic dot in the Atlantic, some 50 km (31 miles) northeast of Madeira, is regarded as one of the best-kept holiday secrets in Europe (see page 57).

- **Levada walks through the island's interior** Don walking gear and head off to explore the island, following irrigation channels which snake their way across Madeira's breathtaking and vertigo inducing landscape (see page 67).

- **Madeira's famous fortified wines** Whether it be dry light *sercial*, a medium *verdelho*, a rich *bual* or a dark amber *Malmsey*, it would be a crime not to sample a glass of the island's superb and unique wine while on holiday here (see page 91).

- **View from the cliffs at Cabo Girão** The truly amazing view from the top of Cabo Girão over half a kilometre (⅓ mile) down to the Atlantic is only for those with a head for heights (see page 65).

- **A morning at a traditional local market** Only real early birds will catch the morning fish markets, but others selling fruit, flowers and wicker continue all day (see page 98).

- **The spectacular mountain trail linking Pico Ruivo and Pico do Areeiro** This rocky pathway is the best walk on the island with absolutely breathtaking views from the ridges and peaks along the way (see page 76).

- **Carnival time in Funchal** Life, light, energy and beauty pulsate through the streets of old Funchal on the best party night of the year in Madeira (see page 104).

- **The village of Câmara de Lobos, Winston Churchill's favourite spot on Madeira** The big man brooded here following his defeat in the 1945 general election, setting up easel on the harbour front for a bit of art therapy (see page 28).

- **A toboggan ride down from Monte in a wicker basket!** A novel if sometimes white-knuckle ride in a wooden toboggan down from the town of Monte to Funchal (see page 73).

▽ *The stunning Madeira Islands*

## SYMBOLS KEY

The following symbols are used throughout this book:

ⓐ address  ☎ telephone  ☏ fax  ⓦ website address
🕒 opening times  Ⓝ public transport connections  ❶ important

The following symbols are used on the maps:

| | | | |
|---|---|---|---|
| 🛈 | information office | ◯ | city |
| ✉ | post office | ◯ | large town |
| 🛍 | shopping | ○ | small town |
| ✈ | airport | ■ | poi (point of interest) |
| ✚ | hospital | ═ | motorway |
| 🛡 | police station | — | main road |
| 🚌 | bus station | — | minor road |
| 🚆 | railway station | — | railway |
| ✝ | church | | |
| ❶ | numbers denote featured cafés, restaurants & evening venues | | |

### RESTAURANT CATEGORIES
The symbol after the name of each restaurant listed in this guide
indicates the cost of a main course meal without drinks:
£ under €7   ££ €7–15   £££ over €15

◗ *Overlooking the town of Caniço de Baixo from the Road to Garajan*

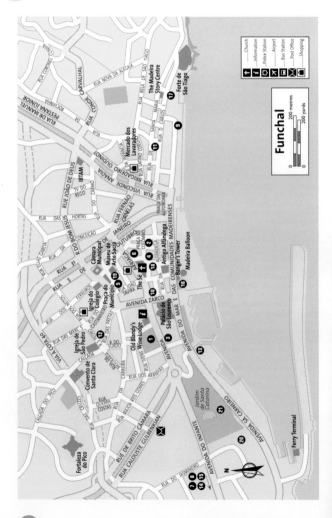

Funchal

0 ___ 200 metres
0 ___ 200 yards

Church
Information
Police Station
Airport
Bus Station
Post Office
Shopping

The Madeira Story Centre
Forte de São Tiago
Mercado dos Lavradores
IBTAM
Câmara Municipal
Museu de Arte Sacra
Antiga Alfândega
Banger's Tower
Madeira Balloon
The Sé
Palácio de São Lourenço
Old Blandy's Wine Lodge
Igreja do Colégio
Praça do Município
Igreja de São Pedro
Convento de Santa Clara
Fortaleza do Pico
Jardim de Santa Catarina
Ferry Terminal

# Funchal

Funchal is the capital of Madeira, and to describe it as the only town of any size on the island is an understatement. With some 125,000 inhabitants, cultural and sporting attractions, and by far the best nightlife, cafés, hotels and restaurants on the island, Funchal is the island's epicentre and the best base from which to explore.

Set in a wide bay and against a backdrop of steep hills which rise into the clouds above, dramatic Funchal has a magical old city centre of basalt and whitewashed buildings, cobble stones, narrow lanes and bustling shops and markets. The centre is divided into three distinct zones: the so-called hotel zone to the west, the centre huddled around the Sé (Funchal's cathedral) and the gritty Old Town to the east. Each has its own particular character: the hotel zone is packed with modern

⬥ *Sculpture near Funchal harbour*

concrete hotel complexes, although you'll also find Reid's there, the oldest hotel on the island; the centre is where most of Funchal's places of historical interest can be found and is by far the liveliest quarter; and the Old Town, the original settlement, is still a working-class area of low-rise terraced fishermen's dwellings lining narrow lanes where life is still lived on the streets and in small bars and cafés.

Funchal possesses the vast majority of Madeira's historical sights, museums, galleries, churches and other attractions, and it would take about a week to get round everything.

The city is also the transport hub for the entire island with buses to and from almost every town and village on Madeira, as well as the ferry to Porto Santo. Two of the best times to be in Funchal are New Year, when the city holds the biggest firework display in the world, and carnival time in late February or early March. With all this on offer, it can come as no surprise to anyone that some 90 per cent of visitors to the island stay in Funchal.

Funchal is compact enough to get around on foot most of the time. When you do have to travel further afield, the city has a superb public bus network operated by Horários do Funchal. Yellow buses run to every corner of the city, and tickets (bought on board or from ticket booths) are cheap. Timetables and route information are available from the main tourist office.

ⓦ www.horariosdofunchal.pt

## BEACHES

Apart from the grubby neglected strip of dirt and boulders near the Beatles Boat, there's no beach along Funchal's waterfront. For sunbathing and swimming, head for the big Lido in the hotel zone.

**Lido** ⓐ Rua Gorgulho ⓣ 291 762 217 ⓛ 08.30–19.00 ⓝ Bus 6
ⓘ Admission charge

◆ Funchal's Town Hall square

RESORTS

## THINGS TO SEE & DO

### The Madeira Story Centre
Opened in April 2005, Funchal's newest purpose-built tourist attraction relates the history and development of Madeira through interactive audiovisual exhibits and classic museum artefacts. The centre not only provides an imaginative overview of the island's past in general, but also tells the stories of some of the individuals (Columbus, Napoleon, Churchill) who have spent time here. It is the nearest Madeira gets to a national museum.

ⓐ Rua D. Carlos I 27-29 ⓣ 291 000 770 ⓦ www.storycentre.com
ⓔ info@storycentre.com ⓛ 10.00–18.00 ⓝ Any city bus heading for Praça da Autonomia ⓘ Last entrance at 18.00. Admission charge

### Praça do Município (The Municipal Square)
This is Funchal's grandest square and the true centre of the city. Centred around a large fountain, its black-and-white cobbles fan out to three of the city's historical buildings. The **Câmara Municipal** (Town Hall) dates from 1758 and has a beautiful *azulejos*-lined courtyard. To the right of that is the **Igreja do Colégio** (Jesuit Church) built in the early 17th century. The interior is a Baroque riot of ornate gilt altars, painted woodwork, *azulejos* tiles and Mudejar-style murals. The **Museu de Arte Sacra** (Sacred Art Museum) located on the south side of the square houses an extensive collection of works by Flemish masters, dating from the 15th and 16th centuries, in the former bishop's palace.
**Museu de Arte Sacra** ⓐ Rua do Bispo 21 ⓣ 291 228 900 ⓛ 10.00–12.30, 14.30–18.00 Tues–Sat ⓘ Admission charge

### Avenida do Mar (Seafront)
This long thoroughfare stretches the entire length of Funchal's seafront and is the focus of much activity of interest to visitors. The quicker you learn how to use this strip of Funchal, the easier your visit to Madeira will be. Here you will find the **Madeira Balloon**, the Beatles Boat and many other cafés and restaurants, the Casa do Turista, the Marina and,

perhaps most importantly, bus stops where services to every corner of the island, including the airport, arrive and depart. East of the busy Praça da Autonomia it becomes the Avenida Comunidades Madeirenses where you'll discover the lower cable car station to Monte and more bus stations. The whole stretch is always buzzing with tourists, locals, cars, buses and street cafés, and 99 per cent of all visitors to Madeira will find themselves here at some point, even if it is just to change buses.

Avenida do Mar boasts some of Funchal's most important historical buildings. The bulky whitewashed **Palácio de São Lourenço** near the Marina was Funchal's first fortress, built in the early 16th century. It now serves as the residence of the Prime Minister of the Autonomous Region of Madeira. The **Antiga Alfândega** opposite the balloon used to be the island's main customs house, but today hosts Madeira's regional assembly. Just across the street, the easily overlooked **Banger's Tower**, now just a heap of stone, used to stand 30 m (98 ft) tall. Built by a British merchant, John Banger, in 1798 as a crane, it was pulled down in 1939.

🔴 *The Madeira Story Centre is a great place to learn about Madeira*

### The Sé

The stern exterior of this small 16th-century cathedral hides a simple but atmospheric interior with wooden floors, a huge gilt altar and a wonderful ceiling, intricately carved with Moorish designs. Musty with the smell of candle wax and incense, the Sé is best experienced during a service, when there's standing room only.

ⓐ Rua do Aljube ❶ 291 228 155 ❷ 07.00–13.00, 16.00–19.00 Mon–Sat, 08.00–20.30 Sun ❶ Admission charge ❶ Free entry

### Forte de São Tiago (Santiago Fort)

This ochre fort at the eastern end of the promenade was built in 1614 to protect Funchal from pirate attack. It served as a garrison until as recently as 1992, when it was turned into a museum housing an exhibition of Portuguese contemporary art from the 1960s to the present day.

**Contemporary Art Museum** ⓐ Forte de São Tiago ❶ 291 213 340 ❷ 10.00–12.30, 14.00–17.30 Mon–Sat ❷ Bus 40 ❶ Admission charge

🔺 *The fabulous Sé cathedral*

**IBTAM**

The museum attached to the Institute of Embroidery, Tapestry and Craftsmanship of Madeira, which oversees standards in the island's handicrafts industry, has exhibits illustrating the importance of Madeira's artistic heritage and includes many fine examples of local embroidery, tapestry and other traditional crafts.

ⓐ Rua Visconde do Anadia 44 ① 291 223 141 ⑤ 10.00–12.30, 14.30–17.30 Mon–Fri ❶ Admission charge

**Convento de Santa Clara (Church of Our Lady)**

Purpose built as a convent and still home to around 25 nuns, the highlight of any visit is the Church of Our Lady, which has some exquisite *azulejos* tile decoration and also houses the tomb of João Gonçalves Zarco, the Portuguese navigator and explorer who discovered Madeira.

ⓐ Calçada de Santa Clara ⑤ 10.00–12.00, 15.00–17.00 Mon–Sat ❶ Admission charge

**Igreja de São Pedro (St Peter's Church)**

A wonderful Baroque church near the Convent of St Clare with *azulejos* tiling reaching from floor to ceiling and a large gilt altar. The painted ceiling completes what is possibly the most impressive church interior on the island.

ⓐ Rua de São Pedro

**Old Blandy's Wine Lodge**

The British Blandy family are still involved in the wine business over 200 years after arriving on the island. Learn more about the wine making process, the families behind it and the different types of grape, and see the huge oak and mahogany barrels containing hundreds of litres of wine on one of the engaging guided tours, which each involve a tasting session. The vintage room housing some wines from the 19th century is particularly fascinating.

ⓐ Avenida Arriaga 28 ❶ 291 740 110
ⓦ www.symingtonfamilyestates.com/winelodge ❸ 09.30–18.00
Mon–Fri, 10.00–13.00 Sat. Guided tours in English take place 10.30, 14.30,
15.30 and 16.30 Mon–Fri and 11.00 Sat ❶ Admission charge

### Jardim de Santa Catarina (Saint Catherine's Park)

The large sloping Saint Catherine's Park, established after World War II,
extends for 36,000 sq m (390,000 sq ft) from the Rotunda do Infante
almost up to the Madeira Casino. This refreshing stretch of parkland
contains a myriad of exotic plant species and provides a little respite
from the road when walking into town from the hotel zone. The large
pink building at the western end is the Quinta Vigia, the official
residence of Madeira's president.

## TAKING A BREAK

### Bars & cafés
### Jardim Municipal  ❶

The leafy municipal gardens on Avenida Arriaga, resplendently
overgrown with tropical plants and flowers, are the ideal place in the
city centre to picnic on a park bench. There's even a small café (£) in
one corner.
ⓐ Avenida Arriaga

### Café da Praça de Colombo £  ❷

Although it serves good, inexpensive drinks and snacks, the best thing
about this outdoor café is its location on the cobbles of Columbus
Square surrounded by the yellow facades and green shutters of
old Funchal.
ⓐ Praça de Colombo ❶ 291 229 582 ❸ 08.30–21.00

### Café Funchal £  ❸

Opposite the Apolo restaurant is the simpler Café Funchal, which has outdoor seating only (under a large blue canopy), a basic menu and a good selection of coffees and cakes.

ⓐ Rua Dr J. António Almeida ❶ 291 222 290 🕐 08.00–23.00

### Café do Teatro £  ❹

Occupying the last two arches of the Baltazar Dias Municipal Theatre, this trendy lunch and nightspot serves soups, salads, coffees, wines and spirits out on the cobbles and indoors. DJs get this gay-friendly place moving at weekends until the early hours.

ⓐ Avenida Arriaga ❶ 291 226 371 ⓦ www.cafedoteatro.com
🕐 08.00–23.00 Mon–Fri, 10.00–late Sat & Sun

### Leque £  ❺

This small café on the main square is a great place to refuel, whatever the time of day. Its reasonably priced range of pastries, sandwiches, salads, coffees, spirits and *Coral* beer on tap are best consumed outside where you can admire the historical setting.

ⓐ Praça do Município 7 ❶ 291 224 229 🕐 08.00–22.00

### Pastelaria Penha D'Aguia £  ❻

Cheap and cheerful coffee and cakes, with a huge selection of pastries, super-fast service and seating on the street outside in the shade of trees. A great place to put together a superb breakfast for a few euros.

ⓐ Rua de João Gago 6–8 ❶ 291 228 119 🕐 08.00–19.00 Mon–Fri, 08.00–13.30 Sat & Sun

### The Prince Albert Pub £  ❼

A lively Welsh-owned British pub in the hotel zone with Sky Sports, pub grub, British beers and live music on Thursdays. By far the most authentic British pub on Madeira.

ⓐ Rua Imperatriz D. Amélia ❶ 291 235 793
ⓦ www.theprincealbertmadeira.com 🕐 09.00–late

### Pub No. 2 £ ❽

This inconspicuous, low-rise beer hall in the hotel zone, with rows of basic wooden benches and a selection of local and British beers, is difficult to find as there is no sign outside. Look for a single-storey building with a red tile roof opposite an attractive drinking fountain decorated with *azulejos* tiles.

ⓐ Rua da Favila ❶ 291 230 676 ◐ 10.00–02.00

### Grand Café Columbus £–££ ❾

This flashy eatery is attached to the lower cable car station of the Monte cable car. Great for breakfast before a trip up to Monte or for a light lunch.

ⓐ Avenida Comunidades Madeirenses 36 (lower cable car station) ❶ 291 242 170 ◐ 09.00–19.00 Sun–Tues, 09.00–00.00 Wed–Sat
Ⓝ lower cable car station

### Grand Café Golden Gate ££ ❿

This Funchal institution with its outdoor tables on tree-lined Avenida Arriaga, green shutters, wicker chairs and colonial feel is one of the most atmospheric places to eat in town at any time of day. There are pretty views of the Sé from the upstairs terrace.

ⓐ Avenida Arriaga 29 ❶ 291 234 383 ◐ 08.00–23.00

### O Regional ££ ⓫

The best of a bunch of places near the Madeira Story Centre, serving very traditionally prepared Madeiran staples in a light and spacious dining area. The fresh fish dishes and pork medallions with sweet potato come highly recommended.

ⓐ Rua D. Carlos I 54 ❶ 291 232 956 ◐ 11.30–23.00

### Restaurante São Pedro ££ ⓬

This contemporary eatery opposite the beautiful Church of St Peter has a menu heavy with Madeiran specialities and interesting décor. A handy lunch or dinner spot when visiting the Convent of St Clare.

ⓐ Rua de São Pedro 2–4 ❶ 291 222 217 ◐ 06.00–23.00

### Beerhouse ££–£££ ⑬

Housed under unmissable spiky mini circus tent roofs on the quayside, this unexpected brewpub cooks up its own cloudy rye beer, similar to German Weissbier, in large copper kettles behind the bar. There are great views of the Marina, but the food is pricey.

ⓐ Porto do Funchal ❶ 291 229 011 ⓛ 10.00–04.00

### Casa Velha & Harry's Bar ££–£££ ⑭

If it's a bit of respite from the sometimes soulless hotel zone you are in search of, look no further than this quaint old place. Upstairs you'll find a cosy restaurant with an international menu; then retire downstairs to Harry's Bar with its fine terrace and wonderfully overgrown garden. Unfortunately the old townhouse is overshadowed by the concrete monstrosity of the casino hotel next door.

ⓐ Rua Imperatriz D. Amélia 69 ❶ 291 205 600 ❶ 291 205 604
ⓛ 12.30–15.00, 19.00–23.00

### Reid's Tea Terrace £££ ⑮

Afternoon tea on the sun-splashed terrace at Reid's Hotel, Madeira's oldest and poshest hotel, is a quintessentially British affair. The price at around €26 per person may also remind UK visitors of good old Blighty.

ⓐ Estrada Monumental 139 ❶ 291 717 171 ⓦ www.reidspalace.com
ⓛ Afternoon tea 15.00–17.30 ❶ Book in advance

### Vagrant (Beatles Boat) £££ ⑯

Tourist trap or piece of Beatles memorabilia? This plush but ageing boat, now set in concrete on Funchal seafront, once belonged to the Fab Four and now houses an overpriced but popular restaurant. The best seats are out on deck and the menu consists of seafood and international meat dishes.

ⓐ Avenida do Mar ❶ 291 223 572 ❶ 291 220 357 ⓛ 12.00–16.00, 18.00–23.00

## AFTER DARK

### Restaurants
### A Tartaruga £–££  ⑰

This simple outdoor restaurant on a charming little square in the Old Town serves up a blend of Scottish (every meal with chips!) and traditional Madeiran fare. The 'Tortoise' was voted Madeiran Restaurant of the Year in 2005 by readers of the *Madeiran Times*.

ⓐ Largo do Corpo Santo 4–6 ❶ 965 709 151 ❷ 10.00–late Tues–Sun

### Apolo ££  ⑱

Munch on meat and seafood dishes or just sip a coffee or beer in this long-established restaurant with its interesting if somewhat unappealing art deco interior and great outdoor seating. The huge

🔺 *Relax and enjoy a drink at Apolo*

people-watching potential and views of the busy area in front of the cathedral gates come free.

ⓐ Rua Dr J. António Almeida 21 ❶ 291 220 099 ◕ 08.00–23.00

## Café do Museu ££  ⑲
Minimalist black tables and chairs under the dark basalt arches of the Religious Art Museum and a menu of trendy international fish meat and vegetarian dishes make this a fashionable if somewhat expensive place for an evening meal or drinks.

ⓐ Praça do Município ❶ 291 281 121 ◕ 10.00–04.00 Mon–Sat ❶ Kitchen closes 21.00

## Night time venues
## Casino da Madeira £££  ⑳
If you feel your holiday has not cost you quite enough, why not try losing some money at Madeira's only casino? Blame the design of this concrete upside-down lampshade on Oscar Niemeyer, the architect who designed Brazil's official capital, Brasilia. It is owned by the Pestana group that seems to run half of the hotels on Madeira.

ⓐ Rua Imperatriz D. Amélia 55 ❶ 291 209 100
ⓦ www.casinodamadeira.com ◕ 16.00–04.00

## Vespas £££  ㉑
A warehouse-like club near the docks and possibly Madeira's liveliest nightlife spot.

ⓐ Avenida Sá Carneiro 7 ❶ 291 234 800 ⓦ www.discotecavespas.com
◕ 00.00–05.30 Wed, 00.00–07.00 Fri & Sat

# Câmara de Lobos

The quaint, traditional fishing village of Câmara de Lobos, around 7 km (4½ miles) from central Funchal, is a popular place among tourists, though very few people actually stay there. Its two claims to fame are as the centre of the *espada* (scabbard fish) fishing industry and as the place Winston Churchill graced with easel and brush during his stay on the island. Nearby are the towering cliffs at Cabo Girão (see page 65).

The main attractions in Câmara de Lobos are the picturesque harbour where colourful fishing boats are hauled onto the rocky beach, and the narrow village streets, usually filled with off-duty fishermen. You'll have to get up pretty early to see the *espada* catch being brought in and sold at the harbour side fish market, but the village's two interesting churches, the harbour and a couple of interesting eateries can be visited any time.

Apart from fishing, this is also one of the centres of wine production on the island, and a traditional wine festival takes place here in early September. It is also home to *Poncha*, an alcoholic brew made of lemon juice, honey and sugarcane spirit. Despite tourism and fishing, Câmara de Lobos remains a relatively poor place where fishermen try to forget about their lifelong struggle with the elusive scabbard through heavy drinking and sometimes very high-spirited card games.

## THINGS TO SEE & DO

### Harbour

With its whitewashed houses, boats of all shapes and sizes resting on the beach and rocky backdrop, it's immediately obvious why Churchill picked this spot to paint. Embarrassingly photogenic, it's also the best spot for a picnic or an afternoon in the company of a glass of Madeira wine and a good book.

⬥ *Picturesque Câmara de Lobos*

### Capela Nossa Senhora da Conceição (Chapel of Our Lady)

This petite chapel on the quayside was originally built by fishermen with stones taken from the beach. Its modest but beautiful interior boasts painted wood panelling depicting scenes from the life of St Nicholas and a large altar. Fishermen can be seen here before and after venturing out onto the Atlantic praying or giving thanks for safe deliverance and a bountiful catch.

ⓐ Rua da Nossa Senhora da Conceição

### Igreja de São Sebastião (St Sebastian Church)

Located on the recently renovated Largo da República square, the whitewashed Church of St Sebastian has a baroque interior with traditional chandeliers, a painted ceiling and customary *azulejos* decoration.

ⓐ Rua São João de Deus

### Henrique & Henrique

At this modern wine lodge just beyond Largo da República square you can sample and purchase some of the finest wines on the island from one of the top producers.

ⓐ Estrada de Santa Clara 10 ☎ 291 941 551
ⓦ www.henriquesehenriques.pt ⏰ 09.00–13.00, 14.30–17.30 Mon–Fri

## TAKING A BREAK

### Bars & cafés
### Amarr á Boia £

A spit-and-sawdust bar on the quayside popular with local fishermen and tourists alike. Best place to knock back some *Poncha*.

ⓐ Rua Nossa Senhora da Conceição 8–10 ⏰ 11.00–01.00

## AFTER DARK

### Restaurants
### Galinha Dourada ££

*Galinha Dourada* (oven-baked chicken) is the speciality dish at this neat, family-run eatery where the wood fired ovens and Madeira wine perfume the air.

🅰 Rua Dr. João Abel de Feitas 59 📞 291 940 642 🕐 12.00–15.00, 18.00–22.00

### Churchill £££

Buses from Funchal disgorge their human cargo outside this most visible of the village's restaurants. A portrait of Churchill greets diners, beyond which they have the choice of a terrace with fine views of the harbour, or an indoor dining room. The menu includes scabbard fish with banana or peach and other seafood dishes, though all the main courses are a touch pricey.

🅰 Estrada João Gonçalves Zarco 39 📞 291 941 451
✉ adelima@mail.telepac.pt 🕐 10.00–22.00

### Vila do Peixe £££

The large, glass-fronted 'House of Fish' enjoys panoramic views of the harbour and Atlantic and is the best place in town for local and imported fish dishes. It's not cheap but it is worth it, and there are even several vegetarian options on the menu.

🅰 Rua Dr. João Abel de Feitas 30A 📞 291 099 909 🕐 10.00–00.00

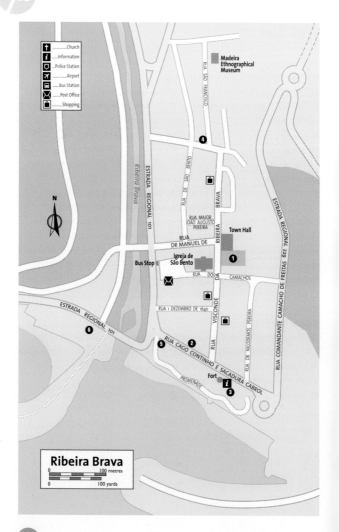

**Ribeira Brava**

# Ribeira Brava

The resort of Ribeira Brava is a busy settlement on the south coast some 20 km (12 miles) west of Funchal. Its name, meaning 'wild river' in Portuguese, refers to the torrent which used to flow into the sea here following heavy rain inland and which created the flat land on which the town was established. Ribeira Brava is well geared up for tourism with numerous lively bars, cafés and a beach, and could make an excellent base for exploring the rest of the island thanks to its transport links. The main tourist sights are the Church of St Benedict and the Madeira Ethnographical Museum, both set within the picturesque web of narrow streets that go to make up the old historical core. The promenade is a modern strip of cobbles and palm trees, alive with outdoor eateries and souvenir shops.

Ribeira Brava was created as a staging post on routes between Funchal and the more remote north, a purpose it still serves today, with public buses to and from places such as Porto Moniz and São Vicente still stopping here for lengthy breaks. The town is a natural transport hub for the island and is very easy to reach.

## BEACHES

In addition to the rocky beach there are manmade sea pools to the west of the town.

## THINGS TO SEE & DO

### Igreja de São Bento (St Benedict's Church)

The town's most visible tourist attraction is this parish church, built in the 15th century, though later given a thorough Baroque makeover. From the outside the most striking feature is its chequered tile roof, while the atmospheric interior is dominated by two huge crystal chandeliers and a beautiful timber ceiling. The original sculpted stone font can be found in a chapel to the right as you enter.

ⓐ Rua dos Camachos ⓛ 07.00–13.00, 15.00–19.00

◔ *Notice the chequered top of Igreja de São Bento's bell tower*

## Madeira Ethnographical Museum

Housed in a suspiciously contemporary looking 16th-century former distillery and sugar mill around 500 m (⅓ mile) inland, this exhibition covering all aspects of Madeira's traditional industries (fishing, farming, weaving, wine and sugar production, embroidery and the manufacture of wickerware) is worth an hour of anyone's time. There are occasional demonstrations of local handicrafts as well as a café and gift shop.

ⓐ Rua de São Francisco 24 ① 291 952 598 ⓛ 10.00–12.30, 14.00–17.30 Tues–Sat, 10.00–13.00 Sun ① Admission charge

## Promenade

The real focus of tourist activity in Ribeira Brava is the recently renovated promenade lined with palm trees, outdoor cafés and restaurants and lapped by the warm waters of the Atlantic. The tiny round fort, the most

◐ Ribeira Brava's seafront

◆ *Ribeira Brava is set in exquisite countryside*

historically interesting building here which dominates the town's coat of arms, now houses the tourist office. Where the promenade comes to an abrupt end at cliffs east of the town, climb the steps to just below the lighthouse for panoramic views of the resort.

## TAKING A BREAK

### Bars & cafés
### Municipal gardens ❶
If it's a shady picnic spot you are looking for, the gardens around the low-rise town hall are the ideal place with their luscious flora and strutting peacocks.
ⓐ Rua Visconde da Ribeira Brava

### Concord Snack Bar £ ❷
Another seafront favourite, the Concord is a traditional type of bar-cum-café with seating indoors as well as across the road. It has the usual selection of coffees, pastries and alcoholic drinks.
ⓐ Rua Cago Continho e Sacadura Cabrol ❶ 291 952 210 🕓 06.00–02.00

### Frente Mar £ ❸
Fill up on cheap simple stodge at this new snack bar behind the tourist office.
ⓐ Rua Marginal da Vila ❶ 291 957 850 🕓 07.00–02.00

### Heredia £ ❹
This tiny open-all-hours Madeiran café is quite handy if you end up waiting a while for a bus back to Funchal. Popular with locals, the outdoor seating on the tiny Largo das Herédias is particularly pleasant. Simple snacks and drinks only.
ⓐ Rua São Francisco 1 🕓 07.30–00.00

⬥ *Splashing about in the waters by Ribeira Brava*

## AFTER DARK

### Restaurants
**Dom Luis ££** ⑤

Possibly the best place to dine on the promenade, this outdoor restaurant serves a selection of traditional Madeiran fare plus pizzas and pastas. The service and views are the most enviable in town.

ⓐ Rua Marginal da Vila ⓣ 291 952 543 ⓛ 08.00–02.00

**Borda D'Agua ££–£££** ⑥

This more upmarket restaurant serves a wide choice of seafood dishes in clean-cut contemporary surroundings.

ⓐ Rua Engeheiro Pereira Ribeiro ⓣ 291 957 697 ⓛ 09.00–00.00

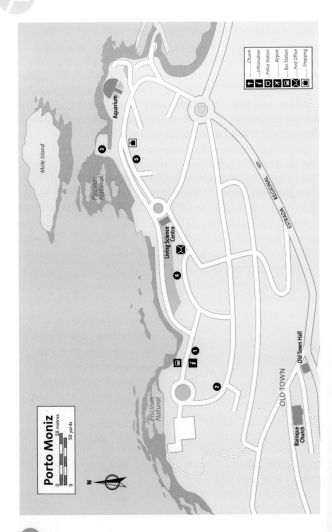

**Porto Moniz**

Mole Island

Piscinas Natural

Aquarium

Living Science Centre

Piscinas Natural

Baroque Church

Old Town Hall

OLD TOWN

ESTRADA REGIONAL 101

0  50 metres
0  50 yards

N

Church
Information
Police Station
Airport
Bus Station
Post Office
Shopping

# Porto Moniz

Tiny Porto Moniz is the main settlement in the remote northwest of Madeira, around 100 km (62 miles) by road from Funchal. With most of the town built on the steep sides of an almost perpendicular hill, the newly renovated seafront boasts two sets of natural sea pools, the main draw here. The aquarium and the excellent Living Science Centre, located here in order to give the place a *raison d'être*, make Porto Moniz a good place to come if you are holidaying with children. Apart from these sights and a handful of touristy cafés, restaurants and souvenir shops, there's not a lot else to see, meaning this distant outpost dies a death when there are no tour buses around. That said, holidaying Madeirans inject a little more life into the place in the summer months. If you are coming to the town on a day trip from Funchal, the three-and-a-half-hour journey through some of Madeira's most dramatic scenery is half the fun. When you get off the bus, the tourist office, with its friendly staff, is located opposite the bus stop.

## THINGS TO SEE & DO

### Sea pools
Porto Moniz is best known for its natural volcanic sea pools located at either end of the promenade. Sculpted over millennia by the sea from porous lava rock, they are replenished when waves crash over their edges. The sun warms the water to a pleasant temperature, creating soothing, naturally-heated swimming pools surrounded by a crust of jagged stone. Those around the Cachalote restaurant are free to enter; at the western end of the promenade there is an admission charge.

### The Living Science Centre (Porto Moniz Centro Ciência Viva)
This unique and rather unexpectedly cutting-edge centre has a range of interactive exhibits aimed at encouraging children to learn about science. There's also a cyber café and shop on site.

ⓐ Rotunda do Ilhéu Mole ❶ 291 850 300 ⓦ www.ccvportomoniz.com
🕐 10.00–19.00 Tues–Sun ❶ Admission charge

## Aquarium

Housed in an old stone fort to the east of the Cachalote restaurant,
Madeira's national aquarium is another attraction even the youngest of
children will love, with 70 species from the seas around the island gazing
unblinkingly at visitors from 12 large tanks.

ⓐ Rua Forte de São João Batista ① 291 850 340
Ⓦ www.aquariodamadeira.com ● 10.00–18.00 ❶ Admission charge

## Old Town

If you can tear yourself away from the attractions of the seafront, Porto
Moniz's tiny but quaint old town clustered around a pristine Baroque
church (surely one of the remotest outposts of Christianity in Europe)
and the old town hall is the reward for the steep climb.

● Old Town, Porto Moniz

## TAKING A BREAK

**Bars & cafés**
**Conchinha £** ❶
Conveniently located beside the tourist office, this is a one-stop-shop for breakfast, a snack at lunchtime and a pizza and beer in the evening. Handy for a refuel before the long journey back to Funchal.
ⓐ Rua Eng. Américo ☎ 969 782 196 🕐 08.00–20.00

**Gaivoto £** ❷
With its menu of pastries, sandwiches, pizzas and snacks, this modern café attached to a guesthouse of the same name is an inexpensive option for breakfast, lunch or dinner.
ⓐ Vila Porto Moniz ☎ 291 850 030 🕐 08.00–00.00

## AFTER DARK

**Restaurants**
**Cachalote ££** ❸
Possibly Madeira's most bizarre restaurant, the Cachalote perches on a platform of volcanic rock amid the town's famous sea pools. Enjoy fish and meat dishes including local specialities such as scabbard fish with banana and rice with limpets in the huge downstairs dining room.
ⓐ Ilhéumar ☎ 291 853 180 🆔 291 853 725 🕐 12.00–17.00

**Mar á Vista ££** ❹
This pricey fish restaurant has a tidy interior and some impressive sea views. The 10-euro tourist menu is quite good value.
ⓐ Vila Porto Moniz ☎ 291 852 949 🕐 10.00–22.00

**Vila Baleia ££** ❺
What it lacks in character this eatery makes up for in well-prepared Madeiran seafood dishes such as tuna and scabbard fish. It also stocks a decent selection of wines. ⓐ Vila Porto Moniz ☎ 291 853 147 🕐 10.00–18.00

# Santana

Lying around 18 km (11 miles) north of Funchal on Madeira's rugged north coast, the town of Santana is the place to come to get your fix of folk culture. Always a favourite among tourists for its photogenic thatched A-frame dwellings, it also boasts the Madeira Theme Park: 7 hectares (18 acres) of land dedicated to the history and folk culture of the island. The best time to arrive in Santana is during the 24-hour Folk Dancing Festival in July which sees the town really come to life. Many may also find themselves here at the beginning or end of hikes across the mountains, as Santana is the nearest settlement of any size to Pico Ruivo, Madeira's highest peak.

## THINGS TO SEE & DO

### Madeira Theme Park
Opened in 2004, this large theme park is an odd mix of Disney World-style dancing characters, demonstrations of traditional local handicrafts, exhibitions on the history of the island and children's playgrounds. There's a hefty entrance fee, a couple of pricey eateries, and it may not entertain the kids as much or as long as you thought. That said, if you are a Madeira enthusiast, and you ignore the glitzy hype, its landscaped parkland and pavilions can provide a long afternoon of fascinating entertainment.

ⓐ Estrada Regional 101, Fonte da Pedra ⓣ 291 570 410
ⓦ www.parquetematicodamadeira.pt ⓛ 10.00–19.00, closed Mon
ⓘ Admission charge

### Thatched cottages
The A-framed cottages of Santana are one of the most instantly recognisable images on Madeira, appearing on souvenirs and postcards across the island. One of the best examples is the tourist office in the park just behind the town hall. Two others can be seen on the same site and house touristy shops. Another large cottage can be found near the turn-off for the Pico Ruivo road and is still inhabited. These specimens

have been spruced up for the tourists, but on your wanderings around the village and surrounding area, notice those still in use, some with their thatched roofs still intact, others with corrugated iron replacements. These are still working pieces of architecture and have probably lasted so long thanks to their roof design, which keeps the rain and wind out well.

## TAKING A BREAK

**Bars & cafés**
**Contradiçoes £**
The nearest Santana gets to a nightlife venue is this smoky spit-and-sawdust pub a few minutes' walk up the Pico Ruivo road. There's *Coral* beer on tap, a few pool tables and an internet room. No food.
ⓐ Pico António Fernandes ❶ 291 573 553 🕐 08.00–02.00

🔺 *Traditional A-framed thatched cottages in Santana*

**Snack Bar Espiga £**
If you've just struggled down off Pico Ruivo in the driving rain, this welcoming snack bar near the tourist office is the ideal place to replenish carbs and warm fingers. Delicious and inexpensive pastries, soups, omelettes, toasted sandwiches, burgers and salads are served with a smile, and the staff speak English. ⓐ Serrado ① 968 842 232 ⓛ 07.00–20.00

**Estrela do Norte ££**
There's a lively atmosphere at the 'Northern Star' where guests munch on international staples at long bench tables in a modern airy dining room.
ⓐ Pico António Fernandes ① 291 572 059 ① 291 573 775 ⓛ 09.00–02.00

**O Pescador ££**
The latest addition to Santana's culinary scene is this chic fish restaurant opposite the Estrela do Norte boasting contemporary design and an adventurous menu.
ⓐ Pico António Fernandes ① 291 572 272 ⓛ 08.00–02.00

**Churrascaria Santana ££–£££**
Located opposite the petrol station where the Pico Ruivo road ends, this pricey place serves up meat and fish dishes in a cosy setting.
ⓐ Pico António Fernandes ① 291 573 879 ⓛ 10.00–22.00

## AFTER DARK

**Restaurants**
**Cantinho da Serra ££**
This gem of an eatery is worth the hard slog 20 minutes (or short taxi ride) up the Pico Ruivo road for its traditional rural décor, real fire and simple menu of fish, roast goat, Brazilian beef steak, tenderloin with sweet potato and the tapas-style dessert tray.
ⓐ Estrada do Pico das Pedras ① 291 573 727 ⓛ 12.30–23.00 Tues–Sun

# Machico

Machico on the east coast was Madeira's first capital, albeit for only a few decades in the 15th century, and is still the island's second-largest town. Well protected by high outcrops of tree-covered rock, it isn't difficult to see why the first Portuguese to arrive on Madeira, João Gonçalves Zarco and Tristão Vaz Teixeira, chose this curving bay as a place to land. The shore is rimmed with a decent pebble beach lined with palm trees, a modern promenade, a marina and several bars and cafés creating a relaxed resort atmosphere. Add to this a smidgen of nightlife, some interesting restaurants, a pretty, historical centre and easy access from Funchal, and Machico shapes up as a worthwhile day trip from the capital, or a place to base yourself for a holiday. Zarco et al landed here in 1419, and still today most arrivals' first glimpse of the island is of the hills around Machico, albeit from a plane window or from the airport a few hundred metres to the west.

○ *Machico is Madeira's second-largest town after Funchal*

RESORTS

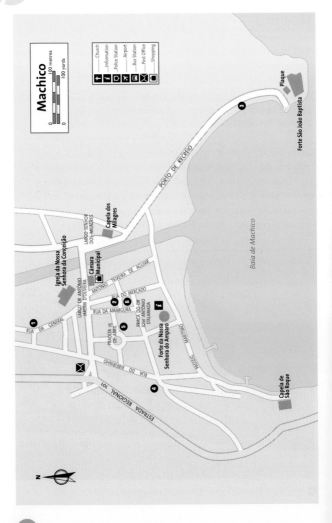

Machico

0   100 metres
0   100 yards

Church
Information
Police Station
Airport
Bus Station
Post Office
Shopping

N

Baia de Machico

PORTO DE RECREIO

Forte São João Baptista

Plaque

Capela dos Milagres

LARGO SENHOR DOS MILAGRES

Igreja da Nossa Senhora da Conceição

Câmara Municipal

ANTONIO TEIXEIRA DE AGUIAR

RUA DO MERCADO

RUA DA AMARGURA

PRACA DO DR. JOSÉ ANTONIO D'ALMADA

Forte da Nossa Senhora do Amparo

LARGO DR ANTONIO JARDIM D'OLIVEIRA

PRACETA 25 DE ABRIL

RUA DA GENERAL

RUA DO RIBEIRINHO

ESTRADA REGIONAL 101

PRACETA

Capela de São Roque

48

## BEACHES

Grey volcanic pebbles and rocks may not seem too inviting, but lying on them is not as bad as it looks. There are sunshades and chairs for hire in summer and exciting views of passenger jets gliding not too far above the sea as they approach the nearby airport.

## THINGS TO SEE & DO

### Largo Dr António Jardim d'Oliveira

The centrepiece of Machico's old historical core is this cobbled square where taxi drivers and locals gather to chat together on benches under giant oaks trees. The area is dominated by the **Igreja da Nossa Senhora da Conceição** (Church of Our Lady) dating from the 15th century with a very loud bell and a disappointingly spartan interior.

### Capela dos Milagres (Chapel of Miracles)

Cross the old bridge over the River Machico to reach the Largo Senhor dos Milagres surrounded by old fishermen's cottages, and boasting this delightful chapel. This houses a much revered cross which was washed out to sea in the devastating flood of 1803, but miraculously found by a passing ship (hence the chapel's name) and returned to the town. Machico still celebrates its reappearance with a small festival in October.

### MACHICO'S NAME

It's widely believed that Machico is named after English merchant Robert Machin, who found himself shipwrecked here with his wife in 1346 after eloping from Britain. Some say Machin managed to get off Madeira on a raft and ended up as a slave in Morocco, where he began to tell his story. News of the deserted island reached the Portuguese court and inspired Zarco to set off for the Atlantic to claim it for Portugal. Romantic hogwash or historical fact — nobody knows.

### Seafront

As in many coastal towns on Madeira, EU generosity has financed the modernisation of the promenade in Machico. Here, however, things may have been taken a bit too far with the new stretch of wavy concrete leaving a slightly soulless impression. The most historical building here is the ochre **Forte da Nossa Senhora do Amparo** (The Fort of Our Lady of Amparo) which now houses the tourist office. At the far eastern end is the tiny **Capela de São Roque** (Chapel of St Rocco) which contains some fine *azulejos* tiles but is usually locked. At the far western end is found

⬤ *Visit the beautiful Capela dos Milagres*

the new marina, as well as a **plaque** marking the spot where Zarco first set foot on this 'island of wood'.

The short climb up Pico do Facho (322 m/1,056 ft), a hill which looms over the town in the west, is a hard uphill grind, but hikers are rewarded with magnificent views of the town and out to sea.

## TAKING A BREAK

### Bars & cafés
### Bar Azul Central da Cidra £  ❶
The pungent aroma of fresh, home-brewed cider hits the nose as you walk through the door of this old-fashioned bar and Machico institution, which doubles up as a wicker shop.

ⓐ Rua General António Teixeira de Aguiar 52 ❶ No tel ● 08.00–late Mon–Sat, 09.00–20.00 Sun

### O Galā £–££  ❷
The inexpensive O Galā is popular with locals, and has a simple traditional interior, great al fresco dining in the narrow street outside and a no-nonsense menu.

ⓐ Rua General António Teixeira de Aguiar 1–7 ❶ 291 965 720
● 08.00–22.00

### Baía ££  ❸
This contemporary café and restaurant has some fine outdoor seating overlooking the bobbing boats tied up in the marina and views back across the bay. Karaoke nights at weekends.

ⓐ Porto de Recreio ❶ 291 966 502 ● 10.00–02.00

### Gonçalves ££  ❹
Fish dishes dominate the menu at this new restaurant just behind the Machico Forum building.

ⓐ Rua do Ribeirinho 1 ❶ 291 966 606 ● 08.00–23.00

## AFTER DARK

### Restaurants
**Mercado Velho ££** ⑤

Housed in the old municipal market, this place has bags of character. It serves up meat and fish in equal measure, which are best consumed in the shady cobbled yard which has tables and chairs clustering round an old fountain.

ⓐ Mercado Velho de Machico ⓣ 291 965 926 ⓛ 10.00–00.00

### Nightclubs
**Discoteca Paparazzi £££** ⑥

One of the only nightclubs outside Funchal. Popular with the locals.

ⓐ Praceta 25 de Abril ⓣ 291 965 387 ⓛ 22.00–04.00 Fri & Sat

⬤ *Machico is set in lush greenery*

# Caniço, Caniço de Baixo & Garajau

If you don't stay in Funchal during your holiday on Madeira, chances are you'll find yourself at one of the many hotels to the east of the city around these three locations. Caniço is a small town with a pretty, historical centre, 1 km (½ mile) downhill from which is Caniço de Baixo (Lower Caniço) where there are yet more hotel complexes, a lido and a beach area at Praia Dos Reis Magos, popular with locals and tourists alike. Garajau is a small town west of Caniço de Baixo where the sole attraction is a mini version of the Christ statue, which graces the skyline of Rio de Janeiro. A large new lido at Garajau, accessible by cable car from the cliffs above, was recently opened. Travel here to enjoy the beaches or seafood restaurants, though otherwise the area makes a rather disappointing daytrip from the capital.

## THINGS TO SEE & DO

### Caniço

The small community of Caniço, approximately 6 km (4 miles) east of Funchal, has just two sights of note. The central square is dominated by the **Baroque church** which, despite its impressive exterior, is somewhat austere inside. Almost across the square from the church is the **Quinta Splendida**, a luxury hotel in the grounds of which you will discover some well-pruned and varied **botanical gardens**. The general public has access to these free of charge. Notice the hotel's swimming pool, which must be one of the finest on the island.

### Caniço de Baixo

A kilometre (½ mile) south of Caniço on the other side of the south coast motorway lies the spick-and-span, purpose built package resort of Caniço de Baixo. The seafront is the chief draw in these parts, and access to the concrete sunbathing platform of the local **Lido** belonging to the Galosol resort is by lift down the cliff face. There's an admission charge there, but a ten-minute stroll east brings you to **Praia Dos Reis Magos**,

⬤ The impressive-looking Baroque church in Caniço

a free beach which has a much more local ambience. There's a snack bar, a public loo and showers, making it the ideal place for bathing or whiling away an afternoon with a big fat holiday read.

**Lido** 🕐 09.00–19.00 Apr–Oct, 09.00–18.00 Nov–Mar ❶ Admission charge

### Garajau

Until recently, the only reason for stopping off in Garajau was to admire the **Statue of Christ**, erected in 1927 on a windy promontory high above the sea. However, the surrounding land has been completely redeveloped. There is now a secluded beach at the foot of the cliff, and the Lido which has appeared there has Madeira's newest cable car – no doubt restaurants and snack bars will follow.

## TAKING A BREAK

### Bars & cafés
### Café de Jardim £
This glass and steel block opposite the Quinta Splendida is good for a quick sandwich or pastry and a coffee after exploring the botanical gardens.

ⓐ Rua Escola ❶ 291 932 937 🕐 07.00–03.00

### A Lareira £–££
Caniço's most convenient eatery is also its best. Located on the square in front of the church, here you can enjoy a mix of Madeiran and international dishes in a rural style dining room with a real fire or just a coffee and cakes in the café opposite, or outside on the pretty square.

ⓐ Estrada da Ponta Oliveira 2 ❶ 291 934 494 🕐 08.00–00.00

### Pizzaria Galosol £–££
Serves inexpensive Italian and thick-base Portuguese pizzas in a mock Italian taverna next to the Caniço de Baixo tourist office. Friendly service and decent food.

ⓐ Apartado 12 ❶ 291 930 930 ⓦ www.galomar.com 🕐 12.00–22.00

## AFTER DARK

### Restaurants

**La Terraça £–££**

If it's honestly-prepared Madeiran fare you hunger for, look no further than this restaurant near the church in Caniço. As the name suggests, the dining space is located on a covered terrace with superb views. Particularly lively in the evenings.

ⓐ Rua João Paulo III 30 ⓣ 291 933 898 ⓛ 11.30–23.00

**Atlantis ££–£££**

A relatively upmarket fish restaurant belonging to the same Caniço de Baixo hotel complex (Galosol) as the Pizzeria. Unrivalled views across the Atlantic.

ⓐ Lido ⓣ 291 930 930 ⓦ www.galomar.com ⓛ 12.00–22.00

🔺 *The package resort of Caniço de Baixo*

# Porto Santo

Measuring a mere 10 km (6 miles) in length and 4 km (2½ miles) across, the golden isle of Porto Santo, washed by the turquoise waters of the Atlantic, is one of the highlights of any visit to Madeira. The principal reason for making the 50-km (30-mile) trip northeast from the main island is for the 9 km (6 miles) of glorious beach which, unlike on Madeira, is warm, sandy and inviting. It's the ideal place in the archipelago for a quiet, family beach holiday. This is a nightlife and package-tour-free zone and hence a place of peace and tranquillity, which may not be everyone's idea of a holiday resort.

Porto Santo is so tiny that the airport runway stretches almost from one shore to the other. Other than the beach and Vila Baleira, the main settlement, there's not a lot else to see, and visitors may be surprised by the barren landscape on Porto Santo when compared with the green and lush overgrown main island. Many arrive here on day cruises from Funchal, sometimes combined with a round of golf at the island's superb golf course. Other activities on Porto Santo include horse riding, watersports and walking, though the vast majority of visitors just head straight for the picture-perfect, sun-kissed beaches to catch some rays.

There are regular flights from Funchal and a ferry link from Porto Santo to the main island. Ferries are operated by Porto Santo Lines and run Wed– Mon with a reduced service in winter. There are five flights a day, operated by TAP Air Portugal (see page 108).

## BEACHES

The real reason to come to Porto Santo is to enjoy the stunning 9 km (6 miles) of Blue Flag beach and dunes stretching from the port in the east to Ponta da Calheta in the west. The sand here, it is claimed, has certain healing properties.

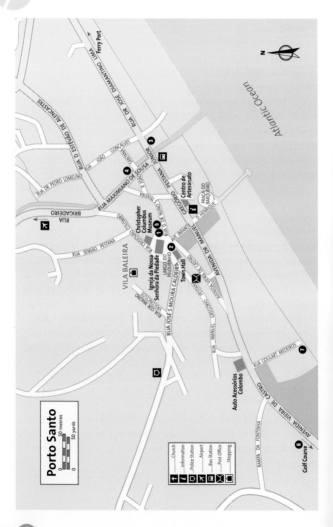

**Porto Santo**

0 — 50 metres
0 — 50 yards

- Church
- Information
- Police Station
- Airport
- Bus Station
- Post Office
- Shopping

Ferry Port

Atlantic Ocean

RUA D. ESTÊVÃO DE ALENCASTRE

RUA DR JOSÉ DIAMANTINO LIMA

RUA DE PEDRO LOMELINO

RUA JOÃO GONÇALVES ZARGO

RUA MAXIMIANO DE SOUSA

Centro de Artesanato

PRAÇA DO BARQUEIRO

RUA BRIGADEIRO

RUA SIMÃO PESTANA

Christopher Columbus Museum

Igreja da Nossa Senhora da Piedade

VILA BALEIRA

RUA CRISTÓVÃO COLOMBO

PELOURINHO

Town Hall

RUA JOSÉ S MOURA CALDEIRA

RUA JOSÉ MANO

RUA INFANTE D. HENRIQUE

AVENIDA DR MANUEL GREGÓRIO PESTANA JUNIOR

RUA MANUEL GREGÓRIO

Auto Acessórios Colombo

RUA COULANT MEDEIROS

AVENIDA VIEIRA DE CASTRO

RAMPA DA FONTINHA

Golf Course

## THINGS TO SEE & DO

Should you get bored of the beach and fancy taking a look around the island, one of the best ways to do so is by bicycle, motorbike or quad bike. All of these can be hired for an hour, day or week from:

**Auto Acessórios Colombo** ⓐ Avenida Vieira de Castro 64 ⓣ 291 984 438
ⓛ 09.30–13.00, 15.00–19.00

By car is also another good way of getting around and there are several car hire agencies at the airport and in Vila Baleira:

**Rodavante** ⓣ 291 982 925
**Moínho** ⓣ 291 983 260
**Auto Jardim** ⓣ 291 984 937
**Insularcar** ⓣ 291 985 319

○ *Porto Santo's stunning beach*

## 4x4 Safari

Another exciting way to see Porto Santo is on a 4x4 safari. These are operated by:

**Lazermar** @ Rua João Gonçalves Zarco 66 ☎ 291 983 379

## Largo do Pelourinho

Vila Baleira's main piazza is a whitewashed and cobbled affair with tall palm trees, giving this far-flung outpost of Portugal an exotic feel. Locals sit chatting on wrought iron benches or in the cafés and bars around the edges of the square, while birds chirp loudly from the trees. The **Igreja da Nossa Senhora da Piedade** (Church of Our Lady) dominates the scene with its clock tower. The exterior sports some exquisite *azulejos* tiles, though the inside is a decidedly unornate affair. The other building of note is the old Town Hall, above the entrance to which the warm breeze rustles the flags of Portugal, Madeira and Porto Santo.

🔺 *Take a break at a café in Vila Baleira*

### Christopher Columbus Museum

Christopher Columbus stayed on Porto Santo in the late 1470s and early 1480s and even married the governor's daughter, Felipa Moniz. The house the couple allegedly called home can be found down a narrow lane next to the church in Vila Baleira. Now a museum, several rooms house a permanent exhibition about Columbus' life, his adventures and relationship to Porto Santo, as well as some temporary art exhibitions.

🅰 Rua Cristovão Colombo 12 ☎ 291 983 405 🕐 10.00–12.30, 14.00–17.30 Tues–Sat, 10.00–13.00 Sun ❶ Admission charge

### Golf course

Designed by none other than Severiano Ballesteros himself, Porto Santo's golf course at the western end of the island is, according to some, the finest in the archipelago. Opened in 2004, it has a total of 27 holes and spectacular views from its greens and fairways.

🅰 Sítio das Marinhas ☎ 291 983 778 🌐 www.portosantogolfe.com

## TAKING A BREAK

### Bars & cafés
#### Apollo 14 £   ❶

A great place to prop up a bar on balmy evenings with hundreds of different tipples available, including Porto Santo's own wine.

🅰 Rua Dr Nuno S. Teixeira 3–5 🕐 09.00–late

### Bar Gel Burger £   ❷

The busiest and best café on the main square. Open all hours dishing up big fat pastries, snacks, coffees and something a bit stronger in the evenings.

🅰 Avenida Vieira de Castro ☎ 291 982 454 🕐 08.00–late

### Café de Cidade £   ❸

The 'City Café' is a very trendy place housed in a modern complex on the seafront. Enjoy pastries, sandwiches, coffees and spirits while surfing the

internet for €2 an hour or watching the huge plasma TV.
ⓐ Vila Baleira ⏱ 08.00–02.00

### Marques £–££ ❹

Join the locals and dine here on inexpensive local meat and fish dishes
followed by a beer or two. Slightly off the tourist trail.
ⓐ Rua João Santana 9 ☎ 291 982 319 ⏱ 10.00–00.00

### Baiana ££–£££ ❺

Next door to Apollo 14 on the main square in Vila Baleira, this rather
touristy and pricey place serves snacks, sandwiches and ice creams, as
well as full-blown meals in a kitschy dining space or under sunshades
out on the square. Large selection of wines.
ⓐ Rua Dr Nuno S. Teixeira ☎ 291 984 649 ⏱ 10.00–late

## AFTER DARK

### Restaurants
### Pé na Água ££ ❻

This popular place, set in the dunes just outside Vila Baleira, is one of
the coolest places to come in the evening to fill up on superb seafood.
Seating is virtually on the beach (the name translates as 'foot in the
water') or in the indoor dining area decorated with maritime regalia.
Chilled music on the CD player and *Coral* beer on tap.
ⓐ Sítio das Pedras Pretas ☎ 291 983 114 ⏱ 11.00–23.00

### Pizza n'Areia ££ ❼

Feast on inexpensive pizzas and salads with the sound of waves crashing
on the beach just metres away at this smart pizzeria.
ⓐ Rua Goulart Medeiros ☎ 291 980 450 ⏱ 10.00–23.00

▶ *Pico Ruivo is Madeira's highest mountain*

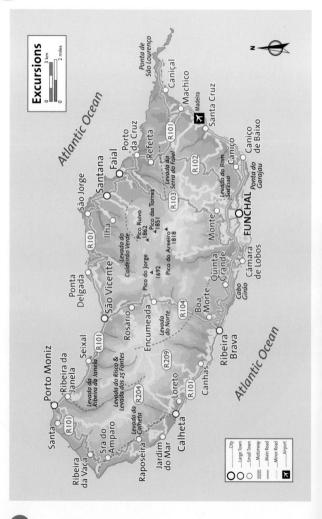

# Cabo Girão

Towering 589 m (1,932 ft) above the sea, the cliffs at Cabo Girão around 10 km (6 miles) west of Funchal are some of the highest in the world. The name in Portuguese translates as 'Cape of Return', as this is as far Zarco got on his first foray along the island's south coast. Cabo Girão makes a fairly good half-day trip from Funchal and is usually combined with a visit to Câmara de Lobos, over which it looms.

Whether you arrive by taxi, bus or private car, you'll end up at the small car park around 50 m (164 ft) from the edge of the cliffs. Walk past the café and waiting taxi drivers through a forest of fragrant eucalyptus trees to the *miradouro* or observation point, which has sturdy iron railings to prevent people falling into the abyss. The view from the top is almost indescribable – looking down, all that separates you and the Atlantic and beach below is half a kilometre ($\frac{1}{3}$ mile) of uninterrupted air, a vertigo inducing vista if ever there was one! It really is like the view from an aeroplane seat. Take a photo with the camera pointing straight down, and watch people back home turn the picture round and round trying to work

⬤ *Don't look down! The cliffs at Cabo Girão are some of the world's highest*

out exactly what they're looking at! Back from the sea there are small terraced fields which are accessible only by boat. To the east you can see Funchal and the mountains behind it, as well as the Ilhas Desertas on the horizon. Otherwise you can just gaze for miles and miles out over the seemingly endless ocean.

Most people combine Cabo Girão with Câmara de Lobos, and an interesting 5-km (3-mile) downhill walk connects the two. Starting just past the Holiday Property Bond complex at the end of a road winding down from the viewing point, most of the route is down sets of shallow concrete steps called the Caminho do Pico Rancho. If you get lost, just ask any passer-by the way. The path is fascinating as it passes through steeply terraced residential areas, giving an insight into how ordinary Madeirans live, how they grow fruit and vegetables, how they channel water down the hills so that it reaches every garden, and the ingenious strategies locals have had to devise to survive in such an environment. The path ends at the road tunnel on the edge of Câmara de Lobos near the Largo da República.

The only public bus to travel from Funchal to Cabo Girão is the 154 operated by Rodoeste. There are currently six buses a day there and four back, taking one hour each way. The service is virtually non-existent at weekends. A taxi from Câmara de Lobos costs around €15.

## TAKING A BREAK

### Bars & cafés

Surprisingly, despite the numbers of tourists who visit the cliffs, the only place selling refreshments is a tiny café at the car park. This is joined to a small free exhibition of historical photos of Madeira, including one of Churchill painting in the harbour at Câmara de Lobos and another of the flying boat which used to link Madeira with Southampton in the early 20th century.

# Levada walks

The *levadas*, a system of aqueducts that crisscross the island, are quite unique to Madeira. These specially-created irrigation channels bring water from the cool wet mountainous interior to the fields and plantations around the coast. They are ingenious pieces of engineering with inclines gauged just right to guarantee a steady flow of water. In the last two decades they have become popular with walkers, as the footpaths that run beside them provide access to some of the most remote parts of the island.

The channels were built by slaves from North and West Africa from the 16th century onwards. Of course, these days modern excavation machinery is used. Digging *levadas* was dangerous work and many slaves died hacking away at the sheer rock faces. They are now patrolled, regulated and repaired by *levadeiros*, who also make sure each farmer gets his fair share of water. From the outset the channels served a dual purpose, not only providing much-needed water, but also serving as the island's transport infrastructure. Only in the last five decades has road overtaken *levada* as the main way of getting round.

*Levadas* are still vital to the Madeiran economy; not only do they supply water to households, irrigate the fields and carry water to hydroelectric power stations, they are also major tourist attractions. Many people manage to organise walks themselves, others rely on the many tour companies in Funchal which take the hassle out of getting to the starting and finishing points of the sometimes remote walks. Always take waterproofs, warm clothes, food and water. Wear sturdy, waterproof walking shoes or boots, and a torch can be handy when negotiating the many tunnels through which the *levadas* pass. The following is a short overview of just some of the best walks on the island.

### Levada da Calheta

Start: Ponta do Pargo lighthouse in the far west of the island. End: Paúl do Mar, a tiny village on the south coast. This is an easy 6-km (4-mile) walk through rural Madeira with views of the Atlantic.

## Levada do Norte

This is one of the longest *levadas* and one of the most challenging to follow, as it has many tunnels and narrow sections along its length. The channel starts at the source of the Seixal River in the north and flows south, ending in Estreito de Câmara de Lobos. This is one of the best places to access its 50-km (31-mile) length for some easier strolls.

## Levada do Caldeirão Verde

Start: Caldeirão Verde. End: Queimadas. This superb *levada* walk arches north below some of the island's highest mountains (Pico Ruivo and Achada do Teixeira). The hike, which takes in some amazing mountain views, is fairly easy going, and the most exposed sections are protected with wire fences. Length: 13 km (8 miles)

🔺 *Levada do Norte is one of the longest* levadas

## Levada da Ribeira da Janela
Start: Lamaceiros. End: Galhano. This picturesque *levada* follows the valley of the Ribeira da Janela River in the far northwest near Porto Moniz. Length: 12 km (7½ miles)

## Levada da Serra do Faial
Start: Ribeiro Frio. End: Portela. One of the easiest *levada* walks to arrange independently as both start and finishing point are served by public bus from Funchal. Great alpine views in the shade of the Laurissilva Forest surrounded by some of the most diverse flora and fauna on the island. Length: 12 km (7½ miles)

## Levada do Risco and Levada dos 25 Fontes
Start: Rabaçal. End: 25 Fontes. A moderately difficult walk with some exposed sections. Admire the forests and waterfalls along the way. Length: 9 km (6 miles)

## Levada do Bom Sucesso
Start: Monte. End: just north of Funchal city centre. This is the closest *levada* to Funchal and its route guides walkers down from Monte to just short of the centre of Funchal. Provides an alternative to toboggan, cable car or bus for returning to Funchal. Length: 7 km (4 miles)

# Monte

The hilltop town of Monte, 500 m ($\frac{1}{3}$ mile) above and 6 km (4 miles) north of Funchal, is possibly the most popular full- or half-day trip for those staying on Madeira. It's an unmissable part of any holiday, not only for its sights, unpolluted air and cooler temperatures in summer, but also for the novel ways the locals have concocted to get you up and down the steep hill between the town and Funchal city centre. There used to be another way, too: a small rack-and-pinion railway which was closed down in 1919 after an accident. Work has started on reinstating the railway, giving day-trippers yet another option in future.

Monte used to be a climatic health spa for high-society guests, but with the emergence of Funchal as the tourist epicentre, the town now plays the role of bridesmaid. One of the most illustrious guests to grace the cobbled streets and squares of Monte was the last emperor of Austro-Hungary, Karl I, who is buried in the Church of Our Lady in Monte.

Getting to and from Monte is half the fun of this day out with at least four interesting ways of getting back down to Funchal. As mentioned, a fifth will open sometime in the next few years, when work on the rack-and-pinion railway is completed. Ascending, there are just two options: bus (Nos. 20, 21 & 22) and cable car. Most choose the latter, leaving from the lower station near the Madeira Story Centre (see page 18) in a modern cabin which glides upwards over the rooftops and backyards of Funchal, then across the wooded glades and ravines above the city. If you suffer from even mild vertigo, take the bus as the view down is sometimes an extremely dizzying affair. The ride takes around 20 minutes and the fare at time of research was 10 euros one way, 15 euros return. These two options are supplemented on the way down by an extraordinary dry toboggan run (see page 73) and a downhill hike along the Levada do Bom Sucesso back into town.

**Madeira Cable Car** ● 09.30–17.45 ⓦ www.madeiracablecar.com

## THINGS TO SEE & DO

### Igreja da Nossa Senhora do Monte (Church of Our Lady of Monte)

The principal attraction in Monte is the beautiful Baroque Church of Our Lady of Monte, which looks down piously on Funchal and the coast from the top of a commanding flight of steps. The almost perfectly symmetrical twin-spired church was built in 1748 after the great earthquake of that year reduced the original chapel to rubble. In true theatrical medieval fashion, this had been built by Adam Gonçalves Ferreira, the first child to be born on the island (his sister was called Eve!). To the left of the entrance stands a bronze statue of Karl I, whose reign began just as his empire was coming apart at the seams during World War I. After the war he went into exile and, having earlier married the granddaughter of the king of Portugal, chose Madeira on which to spend the rest of his days. Unfortunately, he did not have many left and died of pneumonia in 1922, just six months after he arrived. His plain tomb lies in a chapel in the church (on the left), an odd full stop to the centuries-long Habsburg story in the middle of the Atlantic, far away from central and Eastern Europe. The rest of the church, possibly the most important on the island, is a relatively ornate affair with many a Baroque flourish.

### Monte Palace Gardens

A total of 70,000 sq m (753,474 sq ft) of incredible flora surrounds the former Monte Palace Hotel which since 1987 has belonged to the José Berardo Foundation. This organisation has restored the gardens and opened them for the public to enjoy. They are crisscrossed with pathways allowing visitors to get near the thousands of exotic plants from all over the world, which sprout among pieces of sculpture, pagodas, tile panels, Buddhas and rockeries. You could spend all day exploring this place, and some probably do.

ⓐ Caminho do Monte 174 ⓣ 291 782 339 ⓦ www.montepalace.com
ⓛ 09.00–18.00 ⓘ Admission charge

⬤ Climb the steps to Monte's main attraction, the church of Our Lady

## Botanical Gardens

Although not actually in Monte, the Botanical Gardens are linked to the town by a second cable car (ⓦ www.botanicalgardenscablecar.com). This can be found near the upper station of the Monte cable car on Largo dos Barbosas, where bus 22 terminates. The gardens were created in the 1960s by the Madeiran government in the grounds of the Quinta do Bom Sucesso, which was built by the Reid family. Since that time the well-pruned and comprehensive collection of indigenous plants, cacti, palm trees and many other types of flora have bedded down nicely. It is interesting to note that the main south coast motorway tunnels its way directly beneath the gardens!

ⓐ Caminho do Meio ⓣ 291 211 200 ⓛ 09.00–18.00
ⓦ www.madeirabotanicalgarden.com ⓜ Bus: 29, 30 & 31, cable car from Monte ⓘ Last entry 17.30. Admission charge

## Toboggan run

At first glance, the sight of tourists from Britain and Germany being pushed down a hill at considerable speed in wicker baskets by men in straw boaters and white open-neck shirts may seem like something the locals thought up circa 1985 to relieve wealthy visitors of their holiday money. Not so. Horse-drawn toboggans with oiled wooden runners were used for centuries to transport goods up and down the hill between Monte and Funchal, and these have been adapted in the last 20 years to carry tourists. It's a thrilling if sometimes edgy way of ending your trip around Monte, and many cough up the rather hefty €10 per person for the pleasure. The ride lasts 10 minutes and ends at Livramento, where you can find buses into Funchal city centre.

ⓐ Carreiros do Monte ⓛ 09.00–18.00 Mon–Sat, 09.00–13.00 Sun
ⓜ Bus 23 from Livramento ⓘ There must be two people per toboggan

The start of the toboggan run...

## TAKING A BREAK

These cafés are the only eateries you'll find here, so don't expect any plush restaurants.

### Bars & cafés

**Belomonte £–££**

Although the Belomonte fills with underemployed toboggan drivers who in turn fill it with cigarette smoke, this is possibly the best place in Monte for a cheap plate of scabbard fish and other typical Madeiran fare including the interesting-sounding 'pork chop with orange'.

ⓐ Caminho do Monte ❶ 291 741 444 ❶ 08.00–20.00 Mon–Sat

**Alto Monte ££**

Munch on reasonably-priced sandwiches, salads and seafood or nurse a drink on the terrace of this popular eatery above the main bus stop.

ⓐ Travessa das Tilias ❶ 291 782 261 ❶ 08.00–22.00

**Café do Parque £–££**

Tucked away in a corner of Monte's main square surrounded by tropical vegetation and shaded by tall trees, this is the best place in town to grab a quick snack.

ⓐ Largo da Fonte ❶ 291 782 880 ❶ 09.00–18.00

# Pico Ruivo & Pico do Areeiro

The mountain path linking Madeira's third-highest peak with its highest (via the second-highest) is the best on the island, and if you've only got time or opportunity to do one walk, this should be it. The spectacular marked trail constitutes a superb day out in the wilds of Madeira, and due to the easy access these peaks enjoy, you can set off in the morning and be back at your hotel in good time for dinner. Parts of the route feel like a real adventure, though the sturdy wire fences protecting walkers from truly precipitous drops and the well-kept dry stone paths remind you that this is well-trodden ground.

Madeira's highest mountain is Pico Ruivo, which at 1,862 m (6,109 ft) affords views of both coasts of the islands when visibility is good (which it very often isn't). Pico do Areeiro (or Arieiro as it is sometimes spelled) is the island's third-tallest peak at 1,818 m (5,965 ft) and the place the vast majority of hikers start their walks, thanks to its relative proximity to Funchal (a road leads to the top). Between the two rises Pico das Torres, the second highest mountain on Madeira at 1,851 m (6,073 ft). When you consider that this trio of alpine giants are all approximately half-a-kilometre (⅓ mile) taller than Ben Nevis in Scotland (1,344 m/4,405 ft), Britain's highest peak, you can appreciate that this is serious terrain and should be approached as such.

If you are a complete stranger to mountains in general, the best way to do the hike is to join an organised tour (for details of companies see page 86). These are very reasonably priced, the guides are qualified and knowledgeable, and you don't have to worry about getting into the mountains and out again. For anyone with hiking experience, the walk can be done independently, but the logistics can cause a small though not insurmountable problem.

Most start at the café and gift shop at the top of Pico do Areeiro, a busy place in the morning as hikers make final alterations to their kit for the day ahead. The views as you head off for the summit are some of the best, with the russet ridges and dark peaks beyond laid out in front of you. Well-maintained undulating paths take you winding through the

⬤ *Stunning views over the island from the top of Pico Ruivo*

rocky terrain, and the going is fairly easy until you reach the ascent of Pico das Torres. This is by far the toughest section, climbing up almost vertical rock faces with steps cut into them, although this can be avoided by passing through several tunnels. After this comes an easier section, at one point along a narrow ridge chiselled into the rock face, a kind of tunnel open on one side. Next is the ascent through ancient woodland to just below the summit of Pico Ruivo, where you'll find a government-run rest house with coffee, snacks, a roaring real fire and dorm beds if needs be. The short climb from there to the top of Pico Ruivo is worth the effort just to say you've been there, but often the peak is shrouded in mist and cloud. From Pico Ruivo the best option is to continue down a gentle path to Achada do Teixeira, from where Santana is the nearest town.

The walk is around 6 km (4 miles) long in total and shouldn't take more than 4–5 hours with frequent stops to admire the views. Considering it can be 20 degrees cooler at the top of Pico Ruivo than in Funchal, warm clothes and waterproofs are essential. Sturdy walking boots are also a must, and walking poles could be useful. If you decide to take the tunnel route, a torch comes in handy.

## THINGS TO SEE & DO

### Beaches

Some five to ten minutes into the walk, a path forks right off the main route and continues gently downhill to a secluded, rocky beach on the less weather-beaten southern shore. If you've still got energy after the hike to make a short detour, this is an inviting place to picnic, rest tired feet and have a soothing swim before turning back. At Prainha, on the approach road around a kilometre (½ mile) short of Baía d'Abra, you'll discover Madeira's only naturally sandy beach, albeit of the grey volcanic variety. Due to the rarity of such places on the main island, this becomes very crowded indeed when the weather's hot.

Tour groups from Funchal can be found on the route most days, and this is the simplest way to enjoy this exhilarating mountain day. Their minibuses usually head up to Pico do Areeiro via Monte (an incredible,

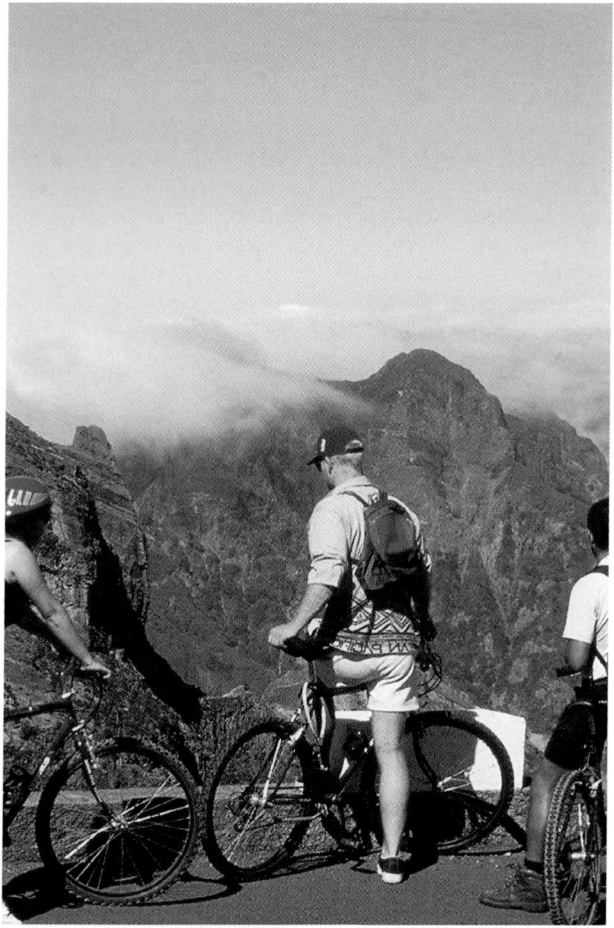

Admire the view from Pico do Areeiro

ear-popping journey in itself) and pick walkers up again at Achada do Teixeira. Sometimes they may include a half-hour stop in Santana on the return journey.

If you plump for the independent option, there are two ways of proceeding. The first is to take public bus No. 56 or 103 from Funchal to the crossroads at Poiso, where the road to the top of Pico do Areeiro branches off the main route north. It's a long 5-km (3-mile) uphill slog to the summit. Having completed the walk as far as Pico Ruivo, either turn round and do the journey in reverse (some do, but it's an ordeal) or get a taxi from Achada do Teixeira into Santana from where buses operate to Funchal.

The second way is to do the same journey by taxi, though this can be expensive. Ask the same taxi you take to Pico do Areeiro to wait for you at an agreed time at Achada do Teixeira.

## TAKING A BREAK

### Bars & cafés

Apart from picnicking along the way, there is the snack bar at Pico do Areeiro's summit and the cosy government-run rest house on the side of Pico Ruivo – a welcome place to relieve aching feet and take light refreshments before pushing on to the top.

# Ponta de São Lourenço

Madeira's most easterly point is the jagged Ponta de São Lourenço (Saint Laurence Point) which juts out around 5 km (3 miles) into the Atlantic. This photogenic peak, made up of a headland and a number of islands, is very different in nature from the rest of Madeira, its arid, rocky, treeless terrain being more reminiscent of Porto Santo. A three-hour linear walk, one of the best on Madeira, takes hikers to the mid-point of the picturesque rocky promontory and back again. Unfortunately, it is not possible to reach the lighthouse at the very end,

🔺 *Ponta de São Lourenço juts into the Atlantic*

⬤ You'll need proper equipment for hiking anywhere on Madeira

as halfway along, this thin strip of rock breaks up into two islands called Ilhéu da Cevada and Ilhéu da Ponta de São Lourenço. The walk is easy in some places, tricky in others, and involves some scrambling over razor-sharp rock with not much between you and sheer drops into the sea – so take care. At time of research, steps were being hacked out of some of the more difficult sections in a health and safety blitz, perhaps spoiling the raw, natural character of the hike slightly. The most dangerous sections are wired off, but fences are in a poor state in some places.

Buses from Funchal and Machico terminate at the car and coach park at Baía d'Abra, a rather desolate, shadeless spot, though normally fairly lively with fellow hikers. The path (officially route PR8) is well marked with cairns holding red and white posts, and starts gently enough. After around 30 minutes it starts to dip into steep valleys and cross thin, exposed ridges before the final and quite tricky section up a steep hill strewn with mud and scree to the highest point, Pico das Gaivotas, and the end of the walk. The views from here are well worth the climb and getting back down is easier than going up. Along the way there are countless opportunities to admire the awe-inspiring sea views, the multi-coloured geological layers within the cliffs, the bizarre rock formations, the turquoise ocean-pushing frothy waves at the promontory and the sheer beauty of the headland which looks like a huge sea creature resting in the water, with only parts of its back exposed. Old lava flows are clearly visible everywhere, giving an idea of the forces which created the peninsula. If you are very lucky, you may even spot a sea lion bobbing around in the Atlantic.

Good boots are essential for this walk, as are a hat and sun block, even in winter. It is also recommended that walkers carry adequate amounts of food and water. Keep to the paths at all times, as all of Ponta de São Lourenço is a nature reserve.

The SAM bus 113 runs direct from Funchal to Baía d'Abra via Machico, though not all services with this number operate as far as this. On weekdays there are five services there and eight back, with a slightly reduced timetable at weekends. The journey takes around 90 minutes. Some travel companies also run guided tours to Ponta de São Lourenço.

🔺 *Rock formations off Saint Laurence Point*

## TAKING A BREAK

### Bars & cafés

Rather bewilderingly, there are no facilities whatsoever at the car park and bus stop at Baía d'Abra, perhaps just a van selling drinks and ice creams. Be sure, therefore, to bring food and drink with you, which you can enjoy at one of the picnic tables dotted around the surrounding slopes affording wonderful views of the Ponta de São Lourenço and the ocean. There are other picnic spots along the way.

# Excursions from Funchal

Funchal is *the* place to join a coach or boat trip to anywhere on the main island as well as to other islands in the archipelago. All public buses start and terminate in Funchal, and you can easily cobble together your own excursion to any of the island's settlements. Organised tour options include boat trips to the Desertas (uninhabited islands visible on the horizon), helicopter sightseeing flights, trips on the touristy Santa Maria de Colombo boat, dolphin, whale and turtle watching trips, sailing trips to the foot of the cliffs at Cabo Girão, diving, sunset cruises, snorkelling trips, rides in the Madeira Balloon, glass bottom boat excursions, rides on the Funchal sightseeing bus, Land Rover safari tours, mountain and *levada* walks, yacht trips and big game fishing. Many operators have booths by the marina where bookings can be made.

EXCURSIONS

**Companies organising excursions and activities**

**Madeira Balloon** – balloon rides 150 m (492 ft) above the city
ⓐ Avenida de Mar

**Sea Pleasure Catamaran** – catamaran trips, sea-life watching
ⓦ www.madeiracatamaran.com

**Nautisantos** big game fishing ⓣ 291 231 312
ⓦ www.nautisantosfishing.com

**Gavião Yacht** yacht trips ⓣ 291 241 124
ⓔ gaviaomadeira@netmadeira.com

**Passeios Virtuais** island jeep tours ⓣ 917 222 589
ⓦ www.passeiosvirtuais.com

**Madeira Explorers** mountain and *levada* walks ⓣ 291 763 701
ⓦ www.madeira-explorers.com

**HeliAtlantis** helicopter rides ⓣ 291 232 882

**Santa Maria de Colombo** sail on a mock Columbus-era galleon
ⓣ 291 220 327

**Ventura do Mar** boat trips to the Desertas ⓦ www.venturadomar.com

**MJ Tours** mountain and *levada* walks ⓣ 291 741 412
ⓔ mjtours@netmadeira.com

**Funchal Sightseeing Tours** 75-minute open-top bus tours of Funchal
12 times a day ⓣ 966 923 943

▶ *Madeira's beautiful botanical gardens*

# Food & drink

While not recognised as one of the great cuisines of the world, Madeiran food is simple, tasty and made using largely locally produced ingredients. Stick to staples from the island and you will eat tasty cheap meals prepared with love and experience. Naturally, most restaurants and cafés these days pander to the wishes of foreign guests, offering the full range of international fare such as pizza, pasta, chips and burgers. Once the tipple of choice across the British Empire, Madeira wine has been out of fashion since the early 1980s, but is still as deliciously sweet and warming as ever.

### TYPES OF EATERY
For breakfast, head to one of the island's numerous cafés that open early and sell a range of excellent and inexpensive pastries and coffees. Lunch can be eaten at a snack bar or café, and round off the day with a full-blown sit-down dinner at a restaurant. Funchal boasts by far the widest range of eateries and even has a McDonald's and Pizza Hut.

### BREAKFAST
Breakfast at most large hotels will be an international buffet affair with a range of imported cereals, cheeses, cold meats, yoghurt, bread and some locally grown fruit. Madeirans like to start the day with pastries, washed down with a cup of milky coffee or hot chocolate. Custard tarts sprinkled with cinnamon, called *pastel de nata*, are the best and most traditional, though there are many other types to choose from.

### LUNCH
Lunch these days is a quick affair, usually just a bowl of soup (tomato, cabbage or bean), a salad, a piece of pizza or a sandwich made with *bolo de caco*, bread containing flour and sweet potato.

◆ *Fresh fruit and veg at Mercado dos Lavradores*

## DINNER

At dinner, the main meal of the day for most tourists, the choice is large. Excellent fresh seafood such as tuna and scabbard fish are the obvious dishes to try. Scabbard is harvested in deep waters (up to 1.5 km/1 mile) at night using long lines. It tastes great but, with its black slithery body, big spiky teeth and huge eyes, looks exceptionally ugly when seen on a slab in the local fish market. Dried codfish, which lends some supermarkets on the island a rather pungent odour, are another local speciality. Fish dishes are usually grilled or fried and seasoned with fennel, chilli, lemon, garlic and laurel leaves. Scabbard is very often accompanied with banana and occasionally with passion fruit. Apart from limpet and squid, seafood has to be imported and is therefore pricey, with some ingredients brought in from as far as Mozambique!

Meat is also popular, but animals may not have been reared on Madeira. *Espetada* made from chicken or pork is meat on a spit, and

◉ *Garlic and chillis at Mercado dos Lavradores*

made properly it should be seasoned with laurel leaves and cooked over a fragrant wood fire, rather like *shashliki* in Russia. The skewer is often hung on a metal contraption attached to the table. Popular side dishes include chips, potatoes, rice, simple salads and polenta.

## DESSERTS

Madeira's signature dessert is *bolo de mel* which is often translated for convenience's sake as honey cake. It is in fact made with *mel de cana* (sugar cane honey/molasses), flour, nuts, almonds, dried fruit and spices. The result is something between British Christmas pudding and ginger cake and it is absolutely delicious (and rather addictive), especially with a glass of Madeira wine. It should be noted that this is *not* Madeira cake, a British invention which could not be more different. Madeira cake or sponge only got its name as it was traditionally eaten in Britain as an accompaniment to Madeira wine.

Pastries and ice cream are other common desserts, as are locally grown bananas, papaya, passion fruit, mangos, oranges, lemons, cherries and apricots. These are often available in some form in restaurants, but self-caterers should head to Funchal's Mercado Dos Lavradores to buy fresh produce.

## DRINKS

Coffee is of a very high standard and inexpensive. In cafés and bars staff will happily make it exactly according to your wishes at no extra charge. If you want black coffee, pipe up early, otherwise milk will be added. Tea is widely available, but is not as good or diverse as the coffee on offer. Local beers are *Coral* and *Zarco* and both are very quaffable brews. Many international brands such as Guinness® and Budweiser are available in pubs and bars frequented by tourists and ex-pats. Madeira has some dubious firewaters made from seemingly anything that grows on the island. Banana, sugar cane, passion fruit, lemon and nut liquors are all headache-inducing concoctions and should be consumed in moderation.

Of course Madeira is most celebrated for its unique fortified wines which are available at almost every eatery. The four types are *sercial* (dry), *verdelho* (medium dry), *bual* (sweet) and *Malmsey* (sweet). *Sercial* and *verdelho* are drunk as aperitifs, *bual* and *Malmsey* are taken after dinner. The older the wine, the better it is, and decades-old bottles are sold at the top wine lodges for large sums. The best advice if you do not have thousands of euros to spend is to leave the cheap three- and five-year-olds on the shelf, and go for a ten- or fifteen-year-old vintage. Only from this age onwards can the wine be called a true Madeiran.

## RESTAURANT ETIQUETTE

Restaurants differ little from those on mainland Europe – choose from the menu, order your food, eat, pay the bill. Tips are not expected, and waiters are not usually overbearing. It very often happens that the dishes you choose from the menu are not available so have a back-up ready. Half portions are available at many restaurants.

When eating out on Madeira, make sure that the only dishes brought to your table are those you order. A mini-scam operated in some of the more touristy parts of the island involves bringing bread and an array of spreads, butter and olive oils to your table immediately after you order a meal. Some holidaymakers have reported paying as much as 3–5 euros for items that were left on the table, but not touched. If bread or anything else is placed on your table during the meal, ascertain whether it is complimentary, and if it isn't (and you don't want it), ask for it to be removed immediately.

# Menu decoder

It would be a foolish Madeiran restaurant that did not have an English translation of its menu available. Small cafés and bars, however, may not.

**Typical Portuguese/Madeiran food**
**Prato do dia** – Dish of the day
**Bacalhau** – Cod
**Atum** – Tuna
**Espada** – Scabbard fish
**Espetada** – Meat grilled on a skewer
**Bife** – Steak
**Caldeirada** – Fish stew
**Caldo verde** – Cabbage soup
**Feijão** – Beans
**Frango** – Chicken
**Marisco** – Seafood
**Porco** – Pork
**Milho frito** – Fried polenta
**Salmão** – Salmon
**Ovos** – Eggs
**Peixe** – Fish
**Pão** – Bread
**Pão com alho** – Garlic bread
**Queijo** – Cheese
**Sopa** – Soup

**Side dishes**
**Batatas** – Potatoes
**Massa** – Pasta
**Salada** – Salad
**Legumes** – Vegetables

**Batatas fritas** – Chips/fries
**Arroz** – Rice
**Azeitonas** – Olives

**Desserts**
**Pastel de nata** – Custard tart
**Bolo** – Cake
**Bolo de mel** – Typical Madeiran honey cake
**Fruta** – Fruit
**Gelado** – Ice cream
**Pudim flan** – Crème caramel

**Drinks**
**Aguá** – Water
**Café** – Coffee
**Chá** – Tea
**Vinho (tinto/branco)** – Wine (red/white)
**Cerveja** – Beer
**Cidra** – Cider
**Leite** – Milk
**Limonada** – Lemonade
**Sumo** – Juice
**Aguardente** – Vodka made from sugar cane
**Poncha** – Lemon and honey liquor
**Inguru** – Ginger

LIFESTYLE

# Shopping

Madeira offers a plethora of potential souvenirs, and countless souvenir shops and stalls in places frequented by tourists mean your suitcase will certainly be heavier on the way home than when you arrived. Wine, wicker, orchids, embroidery, traditional blue-glazed *azulejos* tiles, *bolo de mel*, tapestry, knitwear, liquors and local arts and crafts are all items holidaymakers take home for themselves and their nearest and dearest. On the retail side of things, Funchal has several shopping malls, the biggest of them being Madeira Shopping in the west of the city. Outside the capital this style of shopping is non-existent.

Take care, when buying embroidery, that items bear a hologram proving they were sewn by skilful Madeiran hands and not by a machine in Guangdong Province! Madeirans are rightly proud of their local produce, and anyone selling fake items would be shopped immediately, but you can never be too sure. The following outlets offer the real deal:

## HANDICRAFTS
### Casa do Turista
At first you may think you've wandered by accident into someone's rather old-fashioned house at this museum-cum-one-stop-shop for all your souvenir needs. Tables are laid with beautiful Madeiran embroidery and ceramics, and there are glass cases heaving with traditional handicrafts throughout the many rooms. Embroidery, ceramics, brass, wine, liquors, postcards, guides and many other traditional made-in-Madeira objects can be bought here, but it is also worth a browse just for the spectacle. In the courtyard there is a mock-up of a traditional thatched cottage, and most visitors will be offered a free glass of Madeira wine to loosen purse strings. While slightly on the stuffy side, there's nothing tacky about Funchal's most famous souvenir emporium.

ⓐ Rua do Conselheiro José Silvestre Ribeiro 2 ⓣ 291 224 907
ⓛ 09.30–13.00, 14.30–18.30 Mon–Fri, 09.30–13.00 Sat

⬥ Hand-made wicker goods make nice souvenirs

## WINE

### Diogos Wine Shop

The most central of a chain of shops, the Avenida Arriaga branch of this famous wine shop also boasts an underground museum dedicated to Christopher Columbus. The staff also arrange wine-tasting sessions and talks for groups on the production process, as well as giving expert advice when you are buying wines. All are Madeiran wines which can be tasted before buying. ⓐ Avenida Arriaga 48 ⓣ 291 233 357 ⓦ www.diogosonline.com ⓛ 10.00–19.00 Mon–Fri, 09.30–13.30 Sat

### Old Blandy's Wine Shop

The wine shop attached to the wine lodge is possibly the best place to buy Madeira wine in Funchal. They also stock wines from the Portuguese mainland. ⓐ Avenida Arriaga 28 ⓣ 291 740 110 ⓛ 09.30–18.30 Mon–Fri, 10.00–13.00 Sat

▲ Know your wines

## DELICACIES
### Fabrica Santo Antonio
On the go since 1893, this is a delightfully old-fashioned shop on the corner of Travessa do Forno and bustling Rua 5 de Outobro. The wooden shelves are stacked high with *bolo de mel* of all different shapes and sizes, and other traditional cakes and biscuits. The boxed *bolo de mel* sold here make better gifts than the cellophane-wrapped supermarket versions. ⓐ Travessa do Forno 27 ⓣ 291 220 255 ⓛ 10.00–19.00 Mon–Fri, 09.00–13.00 Sat

## SHOPPING MALLS
### Madeira Shopping
Some 27,000 sq m (294,000 sq ft) of retail space containing over 80 outlets provides the perfect out-of-town mall-style antidote to Funchal's cramped city centre. If you need a retail fix, this is the place to get it, with high street names such as Zara, Mango and Timberland as well as the Portuguese department store Modelo, a Pizza Hut, a McDonald's and a cinema all on site. ⓐ Caminho de Santa Quitéria 45 ⓣ 291 100 800 ⓦ www.madeirashopping.pt ⓛ 10.00–23.00 Mon–Thur, 10.00–00.00 Fri & Sat ⓦ Bus 8A

### Patricio & Gouveira
If you are looking for something a little more upmarket and genuine to remind you of your time on Madeira, head for this huge emporium near the market. The ground floor is mostly given over to embroidery of the highest quality and design; downstairs you will find a fine selection of ceramics, wine, brass and other handicrafts. They even sell whole hand-painted *azulejos* tile panels costing thousands of euros. Many of the items you see here are made next door in the company's own factory. P&G will ship anything anywhere for a price.
ⓐ Rua Visconde de Anadia 34 ⓣ 291 222 928 ⓕ 291 220 898
ⓔ patriciogouveira@net.sapo.pt ⓛ 09.00–13.00, 15.00–18.30 Mon–Fri, 09.30–12.00 Sat

## MARKETS

### Mercado dos Lavradores

Despite the appearance of large shopping centres and supermarkets in recent years, Funchal's old market, housed in an art deco building near in the Old Town, is still going as strong as ever. The building is divided into a section where fish are sold and several other areas where you'll find stalls overflowing with fruit, veg, wicker, spices, wine and flowers. The fish market, with rows of benches laden with scary scabbard fish and whole tuna, gets going early and runs out of steam (and fish) by mid-afternoon. The other sections are open all day and are a vibrantly colourful and aromatic experience. As well as the vast array of exotic produce, many come to admire the *azulejos* decoration of the market building itself.

ⓐ Largo dos Lavradores ❶ 291 214 080 ◑ 07.00–20.00 Mon–Fri, 07.00–14.00 Sat ❶ Opening hours are erratic

🔺 *The popular Mercado dos Lavradores makes for a fun day out*

# Children

It must be stated at the outset that Madeira is far from a children's paradise. Its boulder-strewn, pebbly beaches, resorts full of older clientele, never-ending bus rides, musty wine lodges and all-day *levada* walks are hardly children's holiday material. However, the Madeirans (and Portuguese in general) will bend over backwards to accommodate children and make things as comfortable as possible for you and your entourage. Even if hotels are used to dealing almost exclusively with baby boomers, they are almost always equipped to handle babies just as well. Restaurants will always come up with a special meal for the little darlings if they turn their noses up at scabbard fish, and children love the island's delicious cakes and pastries.

When it comes to things for the little ones to do, the obvious choice is the island of Porto Santo with its wide sandy beaches, where they can bury each other, paddle and build sandcastles from dawn till dusk. Hotel swimming pools and the many lidos around the island are also great ideas, and the **Madeira Balloon** (see page 18) and boat trips out into the Atlantic are sure-fire winners. More specific sights built with children firmly in mind are the **Madeira Theme Park** in Santana (see page 44) and the **Living Science Centre** (see page 41) and the **Aquarium** in Porto Moniz (see page 42). While adults will be breaking out in a cold sweat at the view of the rooftops way down below, children will be enthralled by the cable car ride up to Monte and even more excited by the toboggan ride back down again. Younger children will look in awe at the colours of the island's many botanical gardens, while older kids may enjoy a day in the wilds spotting birds and butterflies. You could even give them the full outdoor experience and camp at the island's only campsite near Porto Moniz.

On a practical note, baby-changing facilities at public toilets are virtually non-existent. The same brands of baby milk and nappies as you buy at home are available in Funchal, though elsewhere the choice will be at best limited. Baby seats are ubiquitous in restaurants and even small cafés. Watch out for alcohol added to dishes in restaurants.

⬥ *The Madeira Theme Park in Santana is a good place to entertain children*

# Sports & activities

## HIKING

This is by far the most popular sport on the island with thousands of walkers hitting the trails every day. Madeira has miles and miles of walking trails along *levadas*, as well as several mountain and hill walks, such as those between Pico do Areeiro and Pico Ruivo, and the linear walk along the Ponta de São Lourenço. There are year-round conditions for hiking on the island, though the weather at high altitudes in the winter months can be cold, wet and unpredictable. At the height of summer low level walks can become sweat-soaked slogs through humid air, though the cool air of the mountains comes as a relief from the baking streets of Funchal.

## GOLF

With the creation of two courses on the main island and one on Porto Santo, golf has also become a popular sport in recent years. There is some dispute as to which course is best, with one camp going for Santo da Serra in the east of Madeira while others prefer Porto Santo. The main asset of the third course at Palheiro is its proximity to Funchal, making it the easiest to reach.
ⓦ www.portugal-golf.info
**Santo da Serra** ⓐ Casais Próximos, Sto. António da Serra, Machico
ⓣ 291 550 100 ⓔ reservas@santodaserragolf.com
**Palheiro** ⓐ Sítio do Balancal ⓣ 291 790 120 ⓔ golf@palheiroestate.com
**Porto Santo** (see page 61)

## SWIMMING

With a water temperature of 18–20 degrees centigrade, swimming and a whole array of other watersports are common activities in the seas around Madeira, though they are perhaps not as popular as some might imagine. There are several scuba diving centres around the island that run PADI (Professional Association of Diving Instructors) courses for beginners.
**Manta Diving Center** ⓐ Hotel Galomar, Caniço de Baixo ⓣ 291 935 588
**Madeira Oceano's** ⓐ Hotel Dom Pedro Baia ⓣ 918 479 922
ⓦ www.madeiraoceanos.com

**Tubarão Madeira** ⓐ Hotel Pestana Palms, Rua do Gorgulho, Funchal ⓣ 965 011 126 ⓦ www.scuba-madeira.com

## OTHER SPORTS

If you are an experienced and very fit cyclist, mountain biking on Madeira can be an exhilarating experience. Sea fishing and tennis on hotel courts are other popular pastimes.

### Spectator sport

The biggest spectator sport on Madeira is football. Amazingly, Funchal, a town of 125,000 people, has no fewer than two teams in the Portuguese first division (which is quite impressive). At present Nacional are slightly better than Marítimo, though both clubs are perennial mid table underachievers. The presence of the two teams in the city means

*Porto Moniz's famous naturally-heated rock pool*

Funchal very often hosts Portugal's most illustrious names such as Benfica, FC Porto and Sporting Lisbon.

**Marítimo** ⓐ Dos Barreiros Stadium, Rua Campo do Marítimo ⓣ 291 708 300 ⓦ www.csmaritimo.pt (in Portuguese)
**Nacional** ⓐ Eng. Rui Alves Stadium, Rua do Esmeraldo 46 ⓣ 291 225 590 ⓦ www.nacional.novamadeira.com (in Portuguese)

## WATERSPORTS

The best time to enjoy watersports in Madeira and Porto Santo is from April to October. However, diving, sailing and windsurfing can be pursued all year round. Hotels, travel tour operators or designated watersports centres can give you details about the best places to go, what's on offer and costs.

A well-known tour company to try is **JCTours** ⓣ (291) 215 100 ⓕ (291) 215 129 ⓦ www.jcmadeira.com ⓔ info@jcmadeira.com

🔺 *Watersports are great fun on Madeira*

# Festivals & events

Just as in Brazil and Portugal, the Madeirans love a party! They will use any excuse – religious festival, public holiday – to eat, drink and dance in the streets, especially in the capital, Funchal. Tourists are always more than welcome to join in the fun.

## JANUARY

Every year begins with one of the most grandiose New Year celebrations in Europe. The New Year firework display is the biggest in the world and now has its very own entry in the *Guinness World Records*™. In 2006 the display went through an incredible 17 tonnes of fireworks with a grand total of 660,300 explosions! It is a truly spectacular sight and draws visitors from all over the world. Getting a hotel room in Funchal over New Year is almost impossible, unless you book months in advance.

## FEBRUARY/MARCH

The biggest festival of the year is Funchal Carnival (February/March). Days before the actual event, lights are hung from the trees, decorations and illuminations are put up, a grandstand is erected along the Avenida do Mar and a stage appears on the Praça do Município. Carnival, which is actually a celebration of Shrovetide (hence its different date every year), lasts five days from Friday to Tuesday, but the main event takes place on the Saturday evening. This is a procession of floats and dancers from the Praça da Autonomia, along the Avenida do Mar, around the Rotunda do Infante, along Avenida Arriaga and ending on the Praça do Município. A rainbow of colours, samba rhythms, energy and light unite to create an impressive spectacle which goes on until around midnight. You may think this is some old tradition dating from medieval times, but the Funchal carnival made its first appearance in the late 1980s and has since gained a reputation as one of the best outside Rio. It certainly is one of the most exciting times to take a short winter break on Madeira.

## APRIL

Two weeks after Easter the *Festa da Flor* (Flower Festival) fills Funchal's streets once again with flower-bedecked floats. Other events (concerts, flower shows) take place on the Praça do Município.

🔺 *Dances are performed at the Flower Festival in Funchal*

## JULY

The most important folk event on Madeira, the 24-hour Dance Festival, happens in Santana in July and sees numerous dance troops performing in shifts round the clock.

## SEPTEMBER

As in many places in the wine-producing areas of Europe, September sees a traditional wine festival which begins in the village of Câmara de Lobos, with events continuing in Funchal.

September is also the month of the biggest party on Porto Santo, the Columbus Week. The highlight of the festival is a re-enactment of the famous explorer's arrival on the island.

## OCTOBER

Machico celebrates the reappearance of a cross which was washed out to sea in the great flood of 1803 with a small festival in October held at the Chapel of the Miracles (see page 49).

---

**PUBLIC HOLIDAYS**
**New Year's Day** 1 January
**Easter** March/April
**Revolution Day** 25 April
**Labour Day** 1 May
**Portugal Day** 10 June
**Assumption** 15 August
**Republic Day** 5 October
**All Saints' Day** 1 November
**Independence Day** 1 December
**Immaculate Conception** 8 December
**Christmas Day** 25 December

---

❍ *Even if you don't know Portuguese, the signs are fairly easy to decipher*

# Preparing to go

## GETTING THERE

### By Air

Flying to Madeira is your only option, as there are no scheduled ferries or boats from the Portuguese mainland (or anywhere else for that matter). The only way you'll end up arriving on Madeira by ship (unless you own one) is on a cruise liner, many of which call into Funchal as part of their itinerary.

**TAP Air Portugal** is the most common livery at Funchal Airport, as the company is the Portuguese national flag carrier, operating flights every two or three hours to Lisbon and Porto. If not arriving from the UK or Germany, it is very likely you will fly with TAP from your own country to the airline's hub in Lisbon, and then change on to a Madeira-bound flight. From the UK, **British Airways** operate daily direct flights to Funchal and **Thomas Cook** have weekly flights, both from Gatwick.

○ TAP Air Portugal is the most frequent flier to Madeira

Many people are aware that air travel emits $CO_2$, which contributes to climate change. You may be interested in the possibility of lessening the environmental impact of your flight through the charity Climate Care, which offsets your $CO_2$ by funding environmental projects around the world. Visit Ⓦ www.climatecare.org

## PACKAGE HOLIDAYS
By far the cheapest way to holiday on Madeira is to book a package including flights, hotel and either half or full board. Travelling independently is certain to cost you more.

## TOURISM AUTHORITY
Madeira does not have its own tourist offices abroad. It is represented by the Portuguese Tourist Board (or ICEP Portugal). Contact their offices for maps and general information about Madeira.

### Portuguese Tourist Board offices
**General** Ⓦ www.visitportugal.com, www.madeiratourism.com
**UK** ⓐ 11 Belgrave Square, London ⓣ 020 7201 6666
**US** ⓐ 590 Fifth Avenue, 4th Floor, New York ⓣ 212 723 0200/99
**Canada** ⓐ 60 Bloor Street West, Toronto ⓣ 416 921 73 76

## PACKAGE TOUR OPERATORS
**Destination Portugal** ⓐ Madeira House, 37 Corn Street, Witney, Oxfordshire OX28 6BW ⓣ 01993 773269 Ⓦ www.destination-portugal.co.uk ⓔ info@witney-travel.co.uk
**Thomas Cook** Ⓦ www.thomascook.com ⓣ 08701 111 111
**Atlantic Holidays** ⓐ 25 Brunswick Road, Gloucester, GL1 1JE ⓣ 01452 381888 Ⓦ www.atlanticholidays.net ⓔ mail@atlanticholidays.net

**TRAVEL INSURANCE**

However you arrange your holiday to Madeira, it is important to take out adequate personal travel insurance for the trip. The policy you choose should provide cover for medical expenses, loss, theft, repatriation, personal liability and expenses incurred due to cancellations. Single trip insurance can now be purchased for just a few pounds or dollars, but always read the small print to ensure the policy covers any activities you intend to do on the island such as mountain hiking and watersports.

**BEFORE YOU LEAVE**

No inoculations are necessary or recommended for visiting Madeira. When packing, make sure to take a good suncream or spray (factor 15 and over), sunglasses, a hat and light cotton clothing. And don't forget your camera whatever you do, as Madeira must be one of the most photogenic places on earth. Otherwise, almost anything you forget at home can be sourced in Funchal.

**ENTRY FORMALITIES**

Portugal is a fully paid up member of the EU and party to the Schengen Agreement, meaning that by default Madeira is too – all good news for most travellers from Europe. If you are coming from another Schengen country, you won't even have to show ID. UK visitors still need to produce a valid passport, as do those arriving from outside the EU (though the vast majority of flights to Madeira originate in the EU). Should you need a visa to enter the EU or the Schengen Zone, contact your nearest Portuguese embassy or consulate.

**MONEY**

The currency on Madeira is the euro, which replaced the escudo in 2002. One euro is divided into 100 cents. Euro notes come in denominations of 500, 200, 100, 50, 20, 10 and 5. There are also 1 and 2 euro coins and 1, 2, 5, 10, 20 and 50 cent pieces.

Use of plastic as a method of payment is on the increase, and most hotels, bar those in the lowest price category, will accept them. Away from your hotel lobby, many restaurants, shops, tour operators and tourist attractions in Funchal will accept cards, but out in the sticks things could get tricky. If card payment is not an option, there'll almost always be a cash machine nearby where you can draw the required sum out in cash. Cards are not accepted when buying bus tickets at ticket booths or from drivers, at the majority of small cafés and bars or at the main market. You cannot pay by cheque on Madeira, except with traveller's cheques, and even these are becoming increasingly harder to use.

ATMs (cash machines) are surprisingly widespread and can be found in even the remotest of settlements. The vast majority accept all major cards, though some limit the amount you can withdraw in one go.

If you have bought an item on Madeira worth more than the rather odd sum of €57.36 in one shop in one day, and you are flying out of the EU, you are eligible for a VAT refund. Visit the Global Refund website to learn about the various ways this can be done, and don't forget to keep all receipts. ⓦ www.globalrefund.com

By far the cheapest and most convenient way to access local currency is to withdraw cash from ATMs using a debit card. If you do bring your local foreign currency with you, change it at any of the many banks on the island or at a *cambio* (exchange office). Changing money at your hotel lobby or using traveller's cheques can prove expensive.

## CLIMATE

Madeira enjoys a year-round mild climate, though the temperature is definitely most comfortable in winter with average daytime temperatures of 20 degrees centigrade. Things get a bit sticky in the summer months, and although the temperature only reaches around 27 degrees centigrade, the humidity can often be quite unbearable. Rain is plentiful and can fall any time from September to June. Sunblock is essential, as the sun is very strong at all times of the year this far south. Don't forget that the higher you climb into the centre of the island, the lower the temperature but the stronger the suns rays become.

Porto Santo has its own specific climate with less rain and more dry sunny days than the main island.

## BAGGAGE ALLOWANCE

As baggage allowances vary between airlines, the best idea is to check your airline or tour operator's website in advance, give them a call or check with your travel agent. Scheduled airlines usually offer higher baggage allowances than package tour operators. British Airways currently allow economy-class passengers a single piece of luggage weighing 23 kg (51 lbs) to be stored in the hold and one piece of hand luggage, measuring 56 x 45 x 25 cm (22 x 18 x 10 inches), which must fit easily into overhead lockers. This includes women's handbags, but laptop computers can be taken on board in addition to your hand luggage. On British Airways flights there are hefty surcharges for checking in more than one main suitcase per person.

⬥ Azujelos *tiles are everywhere on Madeira*

# During your stay

## AIRPORTS

Funchal Airport is a tourist sight in its own right as well as a feat of modern engineering. Seasoned Madeira veterans will relate stories of heart-stopping landings on the old airport's short runway which gave pilots only one chance to land the plane properly. All that changed in 2000 when the decision was made to build a new runway and terminal to allow large passenger jets to land safely. This entailed putting a large section of the runway on concrete stilts over the sea! The gleaming new terminal building handles almost 2.5 million passengers a year.

Despite all this development, Funchal airport is still quite a small affair – so much so, that your luggage may be scraping the sides of the luggage carousel before you've even cleared passport control! On arrival there are plenty of cash machines, car hire companies and all the other services you would expect at an international airport. The departure lounge on the first floor is well stocked with all the souvenirs you forgot to buy around the island, including an impressive range of Madeira wine. There's also a superb viewing platform where you can watch planes taking off and landing at relatively close quarters.

Getting from the airport to Funchal could not be simpler, with three ways of travelling. You could simply jump into one of the waiting yellow taxis which will whisk you down the motorway into town in a matter of minutes for around €25. Alternatively you could wait for the special airport bus costing about €4 which takes around 40 minutes and runs seven times a day Mon–Sat. An even cheaper option is to wait at the bus stop at the far western end of the airport building to catch an ordinary intercity bus. This ticket will cost you under €3, though bulky luggage could be a problem to store. The same options apply on the return journey with the airport bus starting in Praia Formosa and travelling via the hotel zone and Funchal seafront.

**Madeira Airport Funchal** ☎ 291 520 700 🌐 www.anam.pt

**TELEPHONE CODES**

All except mobile numbers on Madeira start with 291 followed by the six-digit subscriber number. As there are no town codes, the full nine-digit number must be dialled every time. From abroad call +351 291. When calling abroad from Madeira, dial 00 then your country code plus the subscriber number.

| | |
|---|---|
| +44 England | +61 Australia |
| +353 Ireland | +64 New Zealand |
| +1 US | +27 South Africa |
| +1 Canada | +44 Germany |

## COMMUNICATIONS

### Phones

There are public telephones in all major settlements across Madeira. Some of these only work with cards which can be bought from cafés, tobacconists and post offices. Many Madeirans now use mobile phones and as Portugal uses the GSM system, handsets from the UK and other countries in Europe will work the same as they do at home. Phones from the US and Canada will not, and Australian and New Zealand handsets may need a change of band frequency. If you have any problems, call directory enquiries on ☎ 118 (automated), 12118 (person) or 177 (international). Remember to omit the first 'o' from the local area dialling code.

### Postal services

There's no real need to look for the post office in Funchal, if all you want to do is send a few postcards home, as stamp machines at convenient locations and postcard vendors sell the necessary stamps for Europe and other places overseas. Post boxes are red in colour. For other services, try the main post office in Funchal.

The postal system in Portugal is operated by CTT Correios and is generally very efficient. Mail from Madeira reaches Europe in around five days, North America and Australia in around a week.

**Funchal Main Post Office** ⓐ Avenida Gulbenkian 3 🕐 08.30–18.30
Mon–Fri
**CTT Correios** ⓦ www.ctt.pt

### Internet access

Madeira is a hotspot in more than one respect – Funchal and most other
communities on the island are peppered with hotspots of the WiFi
variety. For a comprehensive list of wireless access areas, log on to
ⓦ www.wifi-madeira.com. With all those microwaves buzzing through
the fragrant Madeiran air, the locals seem to see little need for internet
cafés, and in Funchal there are a mere handful of places visitors can get
on the web without their own laptops. The most user-friendly and
conveniently located for foreign tourists is **Global Net Café** (ⓐ Rua do
Hospital Velho 25 📞 291 280 671 🕐 09.00–19.00 Mon–Fri, 09.00–13.00
Sat) where they charge €1.50 to use one of their ten computers. Rather
annoyingly (and somewhat bemusingly) they close on Sundays.
The website suffix for Portugal is .pt, and *copy*, *paste*, etc. are easily
decipherable in Portuguese. The Portuguese keyboard differs only
slightly from British and American models.

### Language

The vast majority of Madeirans speak Portuguese. English is widely
spoken in Funchal, though outside the capital few people have a
knowledge of any foreign language.

## CUSTOMS

Goods including alcohol and cigarettes are not subject to any
limitations, as long as they are for personal use. Remember when leaving
Madeira that current security regulations regarding liquids make it
impossible to take wine through customs in hand luggage.

## DRESS CODES

Anything goes on Madeira these days – from full-blown walking gear to
tweed suit and Panama hat. Outside Funchal locals dress very casually,

while in the capital European fashions are more in evidence, and some Funchalese dress in a very smart formal style.

On a more practical note, a hat is definitely a good idea at all times of the year as the sun is very strong, even in winter. Long-sleeved cotton tops are best on hot sunny days. Do not take a trip into the mountains lightly; make sure you pack warm clothes and wear very sturdy walking boots.

Wandering into churches in bikini tops or without a shirt may perhaps raise eyebrows, though it is unlikely anybody will actually say anything to you.

## ELECTRICITY

Madeira works on 220 V AC, 50 Hz. To use electrical appliances from home you will need a continental two-pin adaptor. Laptops from the US using only 110 volts will need a transformer.

## EMBASSIES & CONSULATES

**British Honorary Consul** ⊚ Rua da Alfândega 10 ① 291 212 860–7 ⊙ 291 212 869 ⊜ BritCon.Funchal@NetMadeira.com ① 08.00–13.00, 13.30–15.30 Mon–Fri

### EMERGENCY NUMBERS

**General emergency number** 112
**Police** 291 222 022
**Funchal Police** 291 208 200
**Coast guard** 291 230 112
**Roadside assistance** 800 20 30 40
**Fire Service** 291 229 115

The only Accident & Emergency department on Madeira can be found at: **Hospital Cruz de Carvalho** ⊚ Avenida Luís de Camões ① 291 705 600

**American Consulate** ⓐ Rua da Alfândega 10 ⓣ 291 235 636 ⓕ 291 229 360
ⓛ 09.00–13.00 Mon–Fri

### Tourist information

Madeira and Funchal's main tourist office in Avenida Arriaga does not at first glance seem to have much free information on offer. The staff prefer to keep information safely under lock and key and only hand it out on request. The information officers behind the desks are helpful enough if a touch tourist-weary. They can help with most queries about the island that visitors throw at them, as well as book tickets and give general advice on timetables etc. Many of the brochures they stock can be requested from ⓦ www.visitportugal.com before you leave. There are other smaller tourist information branches at the airport and the Lido.

**Funchal Tourist Office** ⓐ Avenida Arriaga 18 ⓣ 291 211 900
ⓦ www.madeiratourism.org ⓔ info@madeiratourism.org
ⓛ 09.00–20.00 Mon–Fri, 09.00–18.00 Sat & Sun

Almost every village on the island has a small tourist office called a 'Posto de Turismo'. These are staffed by very helpful and informed individuals, though many lack free information. They can usually give you a free town map and generally point you in the right direction.

### Tourist offices

**Funchal** ⓐ Avenida Arriaga 16 ⓣ 291 211 902
**Caniço de Baixo** ⓐ 9125 Caniço de Baixo ⓣ 291 932 919
**Machico** ⓐ Forte Nossa Senhora do Amparo ⓣ 291 962 289
**Câmara de Lobos** ⓐ Rua Padre Clemente Nunes Pereira ⓣ 291 943 470
**Ribeira Brava** ⓐ Forte de São Bento ⓣ 291 951 675
**Porto Moniz** ⓐ Vila do Porto Moniz ⓣ 291 852 555
**Santana** ⓐ Sítio do Serrado ⓣ 291 572 992
**Porto Santo** ⓐ Avenida Henrique Vieira e Castro ⓣ 291 982 361

## GETTING AROUND
### Car

If you are a first-timer to Madeira and plan driving away from the south coast motorway, you are advised to take perhaps a few bus or taxi journeys to see exactly what you are in for, before committing to 14 days' car rental. Many Madeiran roads would be considered too steep to walk up in even the most mountainous of countries. And for every up there's an equally vertigo-inducing down, with a few hairpin bends, rock falls, streams flowing over the tarmac, parked pick-ups and an endless tunnel thrown in for good measure. You'll spend most of your time behind the wheel in Madeira in first gear or with your foot firmly on the brake pedal. If you're a new-ish driver, and you're still not too hot on hill starts, forget it; it's an essential skill on this island. Despite this, road surfaces are excellent, road markings are adequate and Madeirans are skilful and polite drivers.

### Car hire companies
The following car hire companies have offices at Madeira International Airport:

**Auto Jardim** ☎ 291 524 023 🌐 www.auto-jardim.com
**Avis** ☎ 291 524 392 🌐 www.avis.com.pt
**Europcar** ☎ 291 524 633 🌐 www.europcar.pt
**Hertz** ☎ 291 523 040 🌐 www.hertz.pt
**Rodavante** ☎ 291 524 718 🌐 www.rodavante.com
**Sixt Rent-a-car** ☎ 291 523 355 🌐 www.sixt.pt

### Bus
Madeira has an excellent system of public buses which enables locals and tourists alike to reach almost any village on the island within a maximum of 3.5 hours. The service is cheap and easy to use, and services are fairly regular to most places. Coaches run at times when companies expect most people will want to travel, meaning they are geared towards local needs, but on some routes an effort is made to make a day trip possible, with tourists very much in mind. However, be aware that all services run to and from Funchal, and that there are none linking any other two

towns. For instance, there is no bus from Porto Moniz to Machico via the north coast or from, say, Ribeira Brava to Santana via Funchal.

The various bus companies have divided the island up into different sections where only they operate. Asking for information at one company's booth about another company's services will bear little fruit. Tickets can sometimes be bought in advance and always from the driver.

**Madeira's bus companies**
**S.A.M.** – serves the east (the airport, Machico, Santana), green and white livery
**Rodoeste** – long-distance routes heading west (Ribeira Brava, Porto Moniz, Cabo Girão), red and white livery
**Carros de São Gonçalo** – operates services to the west and north (Machico, Santana, Ribeiro Frio), grey and yellow livery
**Empresa de automóveis do Caniço** – serves Caniço and the surrounding villages, grey and red livery
**Horários do Funchal** – Funchal's local city bus company, all yellow livery

## DRIVING RULES & CONDITIONS

When driving on Madeira you should:
- drive on the right-hand side
- keep to the speed limits (50 kmph/30 mph in town, 90 kmph/ 55 mph out of town, 120 kmph/75 mph on the southern motorway)
- sound your horn whenever negotiating a very sharp bend
- make sure your brakes and handbrake are in excellent working order at all times
- ensure all passengers are wearing a seatbelt
- make sure children under the age of 12 sit in the rear seats
- avoid consuming alcohol before driving
- carry a red warning triangle and reflective jacket in the vehicle
- practise your hill-starts if you are a relatively new driver!

If you intend touring the island by public bus, the complete timetable listing every service on the island, obtainable from the tourist office for €1.25, is an essential companion. The bus journey to and from places around the island can be half the fun of a day out, with coaches passing through stunning scenery and along cliff-edge roads affording incredible views. If there are a lot of tourists on board, the driver may even slow down or stop at particularly attractive locations en route. Often the journey can be a bit of a white-knuckle ride with drivers squeezing their old Volvo coaches through seemingly impossible gaps, climbing almost vertical slopes and taking 90° turns around sheer rock faces or atop precipitous cliffs at a breathtaking speed. The bus companies also don't seem to know how to adapt to the new motorway, with most routes doing all they can to avoid it.

**By train**

The only train that ever ran on Madeira was the rack-and-pinion affair from Funchal to Monte, taken out of service in 1939 after a boiler explosion (there are plans to reinstate the line as a tourist attraction, see page 70). Other than that, there isn't one inch of railway track on the entire island, and one look at Madeira's rugged mountain terrain is enough to see why.

**By ferry and plane**

Somewhat surprisingly, public boat transport between coastal towns is virtually non-existent. The one exception is the ferry to Madeira's sister island, Porto Santo, which leaves Funchal early in the morning and returns in the evening. The service is run by Porto Santo Line and the crossing takes around two hours in good weather.

**Porto Santo Line** ⓦ www.portosantoline.pt

Madeira has no domestic air services apart from five daily flights to Porto Santo. The journey takes all of 15 minutes and is operated by TAP Air Portugal.

🔺 *You can travel between Porto Santo and Madeira by ferry*

## HEALTH

Madeira is generally a very safe place to holiday, though there are certain issues visitors should be aware of. Walking in Madeira's mountainous terrain always presents a certain risk from injury and even hypothermia. When heading out into the mountains or along *levadas*, always take warm clothing, whatever the weather in Funchal, and plenty of food and drink. Sun stroke and dehydration are obvious dangers this far south but are easily avoided by covering up, wearing a hat and drinking plenty of fluids. Car accidents are surprisingly rare, though the potential is always there on Madeira's hairpin bends and steep descents. You are not so likely to be knocked down by a car on Madeira as be crushed against a wall or cliff face by a bus. Water is safe to drink everywhere and there are no biting insects to worry about.

Madeiran health care is of a high standard, and should you be unfortunate enough to find yourself in hospital on the island, you will be well looked after. Those from the EU holding an EHIC (European Health Insurance Card) receive all emergency treatment free of charge, while non-EU nationals should make sure they take out the necessary health insurance. If you do arrange your own insurance, make sure you are covered for the activities you have planned for your time on Madeira, such as watersports, mountain hiking, and so on.

## SAFETY & CRIME

As far as criminality is concerned, Madeira is about as safe as it gets, and even the scruffiest parts of Funchal feel far from threatening. If anyone ever did start stealing from tourists or causing trouble in any way, Madeira is so tiny and has such a small population that the person in question would be handed over to the police very swiftly. Madeira is a safe island visited by the type of tourist least likely to cause problems; long may that be the case.

## MEDIA

There are several free English-language publications available on Madeira. The *Madeira Times* newspaper is aimed primarily at ex-pats, though it also contains heaps of information for the tourist, such as restaurant listings and ideas for walks and trips. It comes out ten times a year and is distributed free of charge by tourist offices, restaurants and hotel receptions. The *Madeira Island Bulletin* is a free magazine packed full of advertising, articles, reviews and general information which comes out six times a year. The *Archipelago News* is a free newspaper, slicker than the sometimes charmingly amateur *Madeira Times*, but one look inside will reveal that it contains very little on Madeira, concentrating more on mainland Portugal.

*Madeira Times* ⓦ www.themadeiratimes.com
*Madeira Island Bulletin* ⓦ www.mib.criacoes.com

## OPENING HOURS

Precise opening hours are sometimes hard to pin down, especially when it comes to small bars and cafés. All premises are obliged to display their opening times in the window, but these are often the maximum times they are licensed to open and do not correspond much to reality. Private bar, restaurant and café owners tailor their opening times according to how many guests they estimate they will have. The following should be used as a rough guide only:

**Shops** Open 09.00–13.00, 15.00–19.00 Mon–Fri, 09.00–13.00 Sat. An increasing number, especially in Funchal, now forego the lengthy lunch break.
**Banks** Open 08.30–15.00 Mon–Fri
**Attractions** Open 10.00–13.00 and 15.00–17.00 daily
**Office hours** 09.00–13.00 and 15.00–19.00 Mon–Fri

## RELIGION

Madeirans, like their mainland cousins, are Roman Catholics. Though not the most pious nation on earth, churches are very often full for services, and religious festivals and saints' days are observed with much enthusiasm and partying!

## TIME DIFFERENCES

Madeira, and indeed the whole of Portugal, keeps Greenwich Mean Time. The clocks go forward one hour for daylight saving in March, and back again in October.

When it's midday in summer in Funchal, the time elsewhere is as follows: Azores 11.00, London 12.00, Paris 13.00, Istanbul 14.00, Moscow 15.00, Sydney 23.00, Christchurch 01.00, Washington DC 08.00.

## TIPPING

Tips are not expected and service is usually included in the bill. If you are particularly satisfied with service in restaurants round the amount up to the nearest €5. Leave taxi drivers change.

## TOILETS

Public conveniences are never hard to find across the island and are usually of a decent standard (though the odd nasty place does occasionally pop up). The vast majority of loos are sit-down affairs, though squat toilets do exist. Bars and restaurants do not seem to object to passers-by using their toilet facilities. Men should head for the door marked *Homens*, women for *Senhoras*. Nowhere on Madeira will spending a penny cost you a single cent.

## TRAVELLERS WITH DISABILITIES

With pre-arranged transfers from the airport to a new hotel in Funchal with disabled access and a few well-planned trips by car or taxi from Funchal, holidaying in Madeira with mobility problems is feasible. However, with all these steep hills, cobbles and non-existent pavements around, wheelchair-users may encounter problems everywhere outside their hotels. There's never a guarantee that tourist sights, shops, restaurants and businesses will have any disabled access at all, and a disabled toilet is a rarity. It's always a good idea to phone ahead to enquire about facilities beforehand.

Using the public bus system is out of the question due to the steep steps one must negotiate when boarding. Private transfers are the wheelchair user's sole option.

# SPOT THE BEST BEACHES

Now we help you to get more from your holiday before you've even unpacked your sun cream. Each great pocket guide covers everything your chosen resort has to offer, meaning you'll have so much more to tell the folks back home. We've included everything from the best bars, clubs and restaurants to family-friendly attractions and of course all of those sun-drenched beaches.

Titles in the series include: Algarve, Bali, Bulgaria, Corfu, Corsica, Costa Blanca, Costa Brava & Costa Dorada, Costa del Sol & Costa de Almeria, Côte D'Azur, Crete, Croatia, Cuba, Cyprus, Dominican Republic, Egypt, Fuerteventura, Goa, Gran Canaria, Guernsey, Ibiza, Ionian Islands, Jamaica, Lanzarote, Madeira, Mallorca, Menorca, Mexico, Morocco, Orlando, Rhodes & Kos, Sri Lanka, Thailand, Tunisia and Turkey.

## ACKNOWLEDGEMENTS

The publishers would like to thank the following individuals and organisations for providing their copyright photographs for this book:

Direcção Regional Turismo Madeira 1, 9, 77, 79; Hugo Reis 52, 105; Marcial Fernandes 17, 103; Madeira Story Centre 19; © Dreamstime.com/Mikhail Matsonashvili 87; FLICKR/Vitor Oliveira 15, 38, 50; Pictures Colour Library 20; Wikimedia Commons/Hannes Grobe 98, Barry Caruth 63; World Pictures/Photoshot 10–11, 26, 36, 59, 60, 72; all the rest Marc di Duca

Copy editor: Alison Coupe
Proofreader: Juliet Mozley

Send your thoughts to
# books@thomascook.com

- Found a beach bar, peaceful stretch of sand or must-see sight that we don't feature?

- Like to tip us off about any information that needs a little updating?

- Want to tell us what you love about this handy little guidebook and more importantly how we can make it even handier?

Then here's your chance to tell all! Send us ideas, discoveries and recommendations today and then look out for your valuable input in the next edition of this title.

Send an email to the above address or write to:
HotSpots Project Editor, Thomas Cook Publishing, PO Box 227, Coningsby Road, Peterborough PE3 8SB, UK